The Upside of a Breakdown

The Upside of a Breakdown

A Man, A Museum,
A Mental Institution
and The Power of Resilience

Henry Collins Brown

Wisdom/Work
Published by Wisdom Work

Published 2021

ISBN 978-0-9994813-8-7

Printed in the United States of America

Set in Adobe Garamond Pro
Designed by Abigail Chiaramonte
Cover graphic designed by Freepik
Back Cover photo by Josh Appel

To

Myself

In fervid, if belated admiration
of my many engaging qualities
this volume is lovingly dedicated

Original Publisher's Note

The following note was included in the fourth printing of A Mind Mislaid, printed in August 1937.

When this book appears, the author will be 75 years old, but no one looking at him would suspect it.

A Mind Mislaid tells of a serious and poignant period in Mr. Brown's life. His account of it and of his return to the world of daily life is important, hopeful and inspiring, and shows that no one overtaken by such a calamity need despair.

John Macrae

Editor's Disclaimer: Please keep in mind that the historical integrity of the book has been maintained with original spelling and phrases that may have been worded differently in a contemporary work.

>>>>>>>>>>>>>> Contents <<<<<<<<<<<<<<

FOREWORD

There is an ongoing temptation for many of us who love books to scan the news for the latest titles being published and let them dominate our reading. I managed to break free from that habit years ago, but have fallen into another and better one: Searching out great classics and focusing on them. It's been a wonderful change of pace, and I've learned a lot from an immersion in the great books of the past. It's a practice I'll continue, with new books sprinkled in now and then as spice to the stew. But one thing we book lovers rarely do is look for titles that were published perhaps fifty years or a century in the past and that perhaps never quite became as famous as to count as a classic, but that may be fascinating and insightful in new ways now, bringing us fresh voices from another time.

Not long ago, I was reading some Sinclair Lewis, one of the greats of the early twentieth century. I first enjoyed his *Babbitt*, and then his stunning, *Main Street*. They're both full of wisdom that we need for our lives now. I was getting ready to tackle *Elmer Gantry*, his story about an evangelist who's really a conman. But in the midst of this, my friend Tim Brown sent me a memoir written in about the same era, a mere ten or fifteen years later, by his great grandfather, Henry Collins Brown, the founder of the Museum of the City of New York. The book was first published in 1937. It was a delight and unexpectedly wise. It was a bit like reading James Thurber, or E.B. White, rough contemporaries of Brown. I laughed out loud several times in my first reading of it, and marveled many times more. In these pages, you have his story available once more. I encouraged Tim Brown to make this remarkable account public again so that we could benefit from its lessons in our time.

There was a breezy, straightforward story-telling ability in the era that's refreshing and feels new to us now. The prose of the book flows on like you're having a lively conversation with a very smart and cultured man who has an unusually keen sense of humor in writing about an issue not normally associated with that attribute. Henry Collins Brown isn't reporting here on how he arrived at the idea of a museum to honor the past and growth of what quickly became the greatest city of the world, or how the museum itself was funded and built, which are all fascinating stories in their own right. He's not detailing for us the history of the city's culture, which he did in other books, and very well. He was The Human Interest Historian of New York City in the late eighteenth and early nineteenth centuries and had some intriguing tales to tell about an era that's lost to the fog of history for most of us. But in this book, he's doing instead something very personal, both for himself and us.

The original title of the memoir was *A Mind Mislaid*. It's an account of the author's nervous breakdown and three-year visit to a state mental institution, but it's unlike anything we might expect of such a narrative. The back story is that, after conceiving of the museum and working hard for ten years to get it funded and built, Brown in his mid-sixties was suddenly forced out of his leadership role and replaced by the board he had recruited with a younger man from out west who had never even been to New York City. The shock of this turnabout sent Henry into a steep emotional tailspin and was a blow from which he could not easily recover. He descended into a pit of depression and despondency so deep and total that it was determined he needed the help of a long residential therapy stay for any chance of psychological healing and restoration. This book is an account of his three years encamped amid the people he came to see as his fellow weirdos, psychos, loons, and, his favorite word, "goofs," along with wonderful descriptions of the doctors, nurses, and staff in such a place during the economically challenging late nineteen-twenties and early thirties.

The tale quickly becomes an unexpected story about self-control, a positive philosophy of life, and the emotional resilience we all need as we encounter the ups and downs of normal existence, which is often anything but normal. One of the things the book shows without ever saying it is that overall mental illness, like mental health, can be imagined as falling along a complex spectrum of, for example, a ranking of 1 to 100. A person may be a little off the norm, perhaps at a 10 or 15 on the illness spectrum, which might be barely detectable, or at a 90, in which case he's likely made some terrible headlines and is currently incarcerated for life. The good news to be derived from an understanding that here, as in most things in life, there's a broad spectrum, is that many people who have a diagnosis of mental illness or, these days increasingly, a personality disorder, aren't all hopeless maximally extreme cases, but a great many with the right treatment and environment may regain a proper health of mind and demeanor.

Toward the end of the book, the beautifully recovered author tells us about his release from the state hospital and his research into matters of mental health and healing. He describes a village in Belgium, a beautiful little town of crofters' cottages that is, in its entirety, a place for the mentally ill to go to live and experience a more natural process of healing. He stresses the striking beauty of the place and the way the troubled there are treated like regular people with a wide measure of freedom as they're being helped by the local families of the area who have been trained, often for generations, in dealing with those who may have nearly incapacitating anxieties or depression, or other mental ailments, and how the gentle and positive approach they employ can be so effective.

Some of the main lessons of the book are that we all need to let the past be past, learn to live in the new present, whatever it may be, gain and master the art of emotional self control, and be gentle with ourselves and others who struggle with troubles that in most cases will just be temporary, however long they may seem at the moment to drag on. Time and positive energy can be transformative in ways we often can't imagine. We can bounce back from great difficulties, a human ability for transformation and restoration that I've written about in a book called *Plato's Lemonade Stand.* The same world that has taken away some opportunities that were important to us may yet bring us more other paths forward than we ever could have hoped for or even imagined. This remarkable man's book can restore your faith and calm confidence in even the most troubled times. I am gratified that it's appearing in my Wisdom/Work imprint for the needs of our day.

Tom Morris
Wilmington, NC

>>>>>>>>>>>>>> PREFACE <<<<<<<<<<<<<<

Dear Great Grandpa Henry,

My love letter to you!

I remember hearing about you when family would gather when I was young. We probably met, as I was born in 1957, and you went home to God in 1961, but I was too young to remember and you had a whole bunch of us rug rats around from your children's children. Your creation of the Museum of The City of New York has always intrigued me and "How Cool" was what came to mind as I would reflect on this at different times when I was growing up. Little did I know how your work would impact me at the current stage of my life!

I can remember, like it was yesterday, visiting the museum when I was young for some ceremony and seeing your name in the souvenir store book being sold for the occasion (how cool, I thought again). You would be amazed at how we get our information today on the internet and the world wide web. The abundance of everything available on computers is overwhelming … (more on this in a moment).

My fascination with you and your work as the New York City "Human Interest Historian" continues to grow. You might be surprised to hear that over the past few years we spend time together daily as I read something that you wrote from your 30+ books, and from anything I can find about you or what you documented regarding NYC through Google, on the internet.

A Mind Mislaid is where I started, which has led me to *The Valentine Manuals, Brownstone Fronts and Saratoga Trunks*, and *From Alley Pond to Rockefeller Center*, et al. Before I knew about this last book, I spent two years leading teams on iconic art projects (the Christmas Tree Star and Top of the Rock light sculptures) at Rockefeller Center for the Swarovski Company.

As a result of your work in documenting city history and as the founding father of the Museum, and then my more recent work at Rockefeller Center, I feel very linked to you and NYC in special ways.

So why bring back this empowering memoir about your journey with mental health? What started as an interest in *A Mind Mislaid* has led to amazement about your work documenting so many areas of NYC history at such a special time, and in a unique HCB way. From stories of the centennial of George Washington's inauguration and creation of the Washington Square Arch (see the back cover here), which I learned about in *Brownstone Fronts and Saratoga Trunks*, to the 5 boroughs becoming NYC captured so beautifully in *From Alley Pond to Rockefeller Center*, your work is so entertaining and well done.

Bringing it back to life has become a purposeful passion for me!

Your story about your mental health crash and recovery is very inspiring and I THANK YOU for being so courageous in writing about and sharing your journey. It is well worth hearing for many of us today.

I hope you are smiling down on this project and its chance to bring support and healing to many again just as you did back in the 1930s. With the help of family and friends (Thank you Tom Morris and Abby Chiaramonte), here we are. As the Museum of the City of New York gets ready to celebrate its centennial, it is my hope that many more people who love New York will get a taste of your work as a craftsman of New York history coming to life again to help us build the future from our past!

With much love and affection,

Your Great Grandson
Timothy J. Brown
2021

P.S. As this journey of getting to know you and enjoying your heroic work has grown, I have been thinking of these great quotes from iconic places in NYC and want to share them:

The Quote from George Washington on top of the Washington Square Arch (see back cover) reminds me of your journey to wellness… "LET US RAISE A STANDARD TO WHICH THE WISE AND THE HONEST CAN REPAIR. THE EVENT IS IN THE HAND OF GOD"

Another great one I think you would love is the Wisdom quote looming over the main entrance of 30 Rockefeller Plaza – "WISDOM AND KNOWLEDGE SHALL BE THE STABILITY OF THY TIMES." I stop, pause, and take this in every time I visit Rockefeller Center.

P.P.S. We have decided to partner with incredible friends who are doing important work in the field of mental health. Jeff Sparr and Matt Kaplan founded the PeaceLove Foundation in Rhode Island. Along with their awesome team, they help many people with their work through creative artistic expression. We will be donating a minimum of 20% of our profits from this book to help them with their work.

Thank you again, Henry!

>>>>>>>>>>>>>>> Chapter One <<<<<<<<<<<<<<<

My Mind Crashes

The following story appeared in the columns of the New York Evening Post, April 19, 1929. It was the introduction to an article describing the ceremonies attending the opening of the new building of the Museum of the City of New York, on Fifth Avenue, founded by me and which had just been completed.

CITY HE LOVED LOST TO OLD CHRONICLER
MEMORIES THAT WERE LIFE OF H. C. BROWN FADE,
AS DREAM OF MUSEUM COMES TRUE
NOW A MENTAL PATIENT

Henry Collins Brown has lost his memories—the uncommon memories he lived by, and the memories of Old New York that he marshaled in the easiest of prose, for the pleasure of the City's best people.

All the store of odd fact and anecdote that make the books about "The Elegant Eighties" and "The Golden Nineties," has slipped from the mind of their author, along with the strange lore of the good old days that he revived as editor of *Valentine's Manual.*

In this April of 1929, when the corner-stone of the City's

own particular museum about itself is about to be laid, the man who dreamed this museum is a mental patient in the old Bloomingdale Asylum at White Plains. His mind is disarranged and scattered, like the thousands of odds and ends of the City's past that will eventually be assembled and systematized at the new museum.

Whether the scattered memories of Mr. Brown will ever be reassembled is a question over which the doctors shake their heads. The institution where he rests is backed by the same stalwarts in metropolitan society who helped to finance his curious research into bygone Gotham, and to publish its fruits, with the quaintest of illustrations, copper engraved, but the doctors say that Mr. Brown's interest in New York life has passed with his memories. For more than a year his broken mind has been closed to all news of it.

This sad twilight of the mind came softly over the eager chronicler of old New York at Christmas time, 1928, when Mr. Brown was about to deliver his annual lecture on the City's oldtime Christmas, before the bright tree in the Fifth Avenue home of an international banker.

∽

I did not see this brilliant effusion until quite recently. When I did, it struck me as a very good example of the sob-sister school of journalism which calls for a second helping of tripe in a case like this.

Far be it from me to intrude, therefore, at such a sacred moment, any comment, ribald or otherwise, or even to suggest that this moving tale existed only in the heated imagination of the gifted writer. To deny the truth of the story would be to destroy one of the fondest illusions of the dear public regarding nervous breakdowns. Yet I fear that is just what I will do, much as I may later regret it. For many persons suffer keenly from the mere thought that they are "losing their minds," and as a result, actually do suffer a temporary eclipse of their normal efficiency, thereby inflicting untold misery on all who are near and dear to them. Such persons should not read this book, as they will find that it is not only difficult to "lose one's mind," but also positively impossible.

The personal narrative related in these pages, is by no means unusual. Most persons, however, who have gone through it, are ever after strangely silent upon the subject. Apparently it does not possess the glamor, the exquisite charm, which seems to be the exclusive and peculiar property of, for example, an "operation." Operations have been known to provide practically unlimited material for a lifetime of weird though wholly unromantic reminiscences. Nervous breakdowns, on the other hand, have uncomplainingly taken the place with that pitiful figure in the old song—"Oh, No, We Never Mention Her."

Not only does a recovered patient dread to speak of his illness, but looks upon himself as having brought disgrace upon the family. He would, if allowed, walk only in shady lanes and neglected byways, shunning the highroad lest he be seen of men. There are, of course, occasional exceptions. I am one.

When I "returned to the world," as the hospitals naively put it, I made no secret of it. I spoke out frankly and freely. I wanted people to have all the ghastly details so that if they should afterwards conclude that I had been crazier than they had been led to believe, it would be no fault of mine.

I even had the temerity to address several clubs on this subject. I took for my text "A Mind That Found Itself." I shall always be grateful to the chairman of the first meeting. "I am going to introduce as our speaker this evening," he said, beaming upon the audience, "the only man I ever knew who went crazy and brags about it." At the conclusion of the talk, a dear old lady whispered in my ear, "Don't go hunting for that lost mind of yours any more. You might find it; hang on to the one you have."

The real reason for this book is the hope that possibly I may be able to show the world that a nervous breakdown is not necessarily the end of all things, nor is there any danger that you will never get well. You are in for a pretty bad time; but so you would be if you had typhoid, double pneumonia, or spinal meningitis. Furthermore—and this is the sad part of it, mates—you are where you are largely as the result of some damn foolishness on your own part. I shall enlarge upon this later on.

There is absolutely nothing mysterious or supernatural about a breakdown of this kind. It has a definite reason for existing, the cause of which is easily ascertainable. In my own case it was the loss of the Museum of the City of New York, an enterprise into which I had put the best years of my life, only to be robbed of the results of my labor with success just in sight. To an emotional temperament like mine, that was an overwhelming disaster.

The ambition of my life was now an accomplished fact. The hopes, the fears, the trials and the tribulations of the past were all forgotten in the glorious sunshine of the present. The world was beautiful and life was sweet.

And then I lost it! A younger man was wanted!

I was then sixty-five and without funds; the work that justified my existence lay in ruins at my feet. It was a day of unutterable woe. Had I been younger, or had it not come at the end of a ten-year struggle, which had left me physically and mentally exhausted, I would have weathered the shock all right; principally because there would have been no shock to weather—the Museum would have stayed right in the hands of its creator and founder, where it belonged. My resistance had been weakened to the vanishing point, as the result of the long nervous strain inseparable from such an enterprise, undertaken perforce on a shoe string, and the old fighting spirit was gone. So when I was eased out in favor of a younger man from the wild and woolly West, who had never seen New York until he came to take charge of the Museum, I just naturally crashed.

But all was not lost. Delightful memories still remained. The joy of combat was mine and mine alone. The Museum did not spring armed cap-a-pie from the loins of Jove.

For months at a time the till, like Mother Hubbard's cupboard, was empty and bare. The first sizable check that gave hope almost killed me at the same time. It was for a thousand dollars and it came from Mrs. Carnegie. It arrived on a lovely spring morning, and I had opened all the doors and windows. When I saw the check, I let it fall from my nerveless grasp. An errant gust of wind, from the open window behind me, swept up the check and bore it aloft and outdoors. Up, up, in the sky it flew, across the lawn and over the turbulent waters of Hell Gate! It found a watery grave near Mill Rock. Oftentimes in the hospital I wished I could have joined it.

Yet that tragedy was nothing compared to the loss of the old Vanderbilt Mansion on the Plaza. Mr. Munsey was willing to pay the bill and the home of the Museum would have been in a typical, high-class, residential, nineteenth century, New York house, which was a proper place for it. This would have been in keeping with the old home of the Marquise de Sévigné in Paris which houses the Musée Carnavalet, and the Stafford House in London which houses the London Museum. But the new management had to insult Mr. Munsey, who promptly walked up the street and dumped his millions into an institution whose portals he had never even entered.

I guess I must always have been more or less crazy. I blushingly admit that I preferred to head an organization running on its own private funds to one that depends on public money for existence. Further proof of this craziness will be found in the fact that I also prefer a diamond to a dunghill, which is in my humble opinion the difference between a smug, up-to-date, air-conditioned, streamlined, swanky, beauty shoppe and a historic, nationally known building representative of Old New York that was lost.

Nor will the recollection of that first meeting in the old Gracie

Mansion at which the Museum was formerly organized, ever fail to be for me a gorgeous memory.

The City had just presented us with this ancient home of that fine old merchant of old New York. It was an eminently fitting and proper background. The building had been long unused and was in a deplorable condition. For light, we had only a few spluttering tallow candles that threatened momentarily to leave us in utter darkness; there were some decrepit, tottering chairs, but for the most part we sat on old empty packing boxes and on rough planks stretched across wooden horses that had been used by the carpenters.

Perhaps I should have held the meeting in Mr. Speyer's luxurious office in Wall Street, which he asked me to do. But I had in mind the beginnings of the Metropolitan Museum of Art in a room over the stable of John Taylor Johnston on 8th Street before it moved to the Cuyler Mansion on 14th and before Bill Tweed took hold of it. So I wanted to carry on in the spirit and traditions of old New York. Maybe that was a mistake. But I would do the same thing over again nevertheless.

Those who were present on that occasion have rescued their names from oblivion. The Hon. Murray Hurlburt, acting Mayor, represented the ancient and imperial City of New York.

Judge Ingraham was elected our first president. He has passed on. So has Henry Richmond Taylor, our first treasurer, and William Rhinelander Stewart, one of our first founders, and the Hon. Maurice Block, and Park Commissioner Francis D. Gallatin who procured the Gracie Mansion from the city as our first home. *Requiescant in pace*! Bob Le Roy, our present and original secretary; Mr. George A. Zabriskie and myself alone remain of that original group.

I was very happy that night. The Museum was now a going concern and was bound to be a success whether I lived or died. I had accomplished something for the city I loved. It was a comforting thought.

Whatever regrets I may have had, whatever anger I may have felt, have long ago passed out of my mind. I look upon it now as something that never happened. In a sermon I once heard Dr. Rainsford preach, he said, "No matter how hard it is, we *must* forget; and after we have forgotten, it is not hard to forgive." The night is coming for me. I do not want the sunset and evening star obscured by any clouds of hatred or regret.

There is a marble tablet in the Museum ascribing its creation to a certain member. I often wonder just who was the real "Creator" of this noble institution. I used to think I was. But all I ever did was to originate the idea, and work on it for ten long, weary years before public interest in it could be aroused. My name is signed as President on the contract with the City and I wrote the Constitution and by-laws, now reposing in the corner stone. In association with the late Hon. Maurice Block, Leader of the Assembly at that time, I obtained the final passage of the Enabling Act, after it had failed at two previous sessions, whereby the City was empowered to give the Museum Corporation the land on which the present building is erected and to extend such financial aid from time to time as the City saw fit to give. And when I left, the treasury had a very substantial sum in cash, the project was before the Rockefeller and other important interests, and a complete set of Officers and Trustees elected.

So when I look at this marble tablet, I see nothing but a jackdaw strutting around in the borrowed plumage of a peacock. Perhaps this is merely a fantastic impression left over from Bloomingdale days. And again—perhaps not.

The Museum itself is however a great addition to the cultural life of our City. May it live long and prosper!

And if any other man has an idea equally valuable to his city, my advice to him is to go ahead and do it even if his sole reward be a stretch in a bug house. His city at least will be the gainer and what happens to him personally means not a thing. There is no property in an idea and no short cut to a flood light in the social world equal to that afforded by such distinguished service as "creating a great cultural institution.

Kipling had you in mind when he wrote:

Or watch the things you gave your life to, broken,
And stoop and build 'em up with worn-out tools:

If you can make one heap of all your winnings
And risk it on one turn of pitch-and-toss,
And lose, and start again at your beginnings
And never breathe a word about your loss;

Yours is the Earth and everything that's in it.

>>>>>>>>>>>>>> Chapter Two <<<<<<<<<<<<<<

I Enter "Cuckoo" Land

I am now in Bloomingdale Hospital, in White Plains, New York. The great doors have clanged behind me. The last farewells have been spoken, and I am in the Receiving Ward, alone with my thoughts. The bright, happy world which I left but a moment ago, I may never see again. I have taken the first step in my new Pilgrim's Progress; I am silently praying that God will call me home, ere I take the next.

In olden times it was considered perfectly good form to dig holes in the ground as prisons for such unfortunates as myself, and throw them into it like rats in a pit. It is only within recent years that this problem of mental treatment has become a department of medical activity under the State. Forty years ago this field was occupied wholly by the county authorities. Patients were kept largely in almshouses. Scientific treatment was unheard of. They were the accursed of God and received less care than farm animals. The idea that they were possibly curable, never entered anyone's mind. They were encumberers of the ground, and taxpayers grumbled loudly at their cost.

In all annals of human suffering there is nothing to compare with the agony, the cruelty and horror which was at that time the state of these poor unfortunates. It is a black page in the history of our boasted civilization. Many tearful songs have been written about that sad journey over the hill to the poorhouse, but the worst of these vile places was a paradise of comfort compared with the wretched hovels that hid from public view the pitiable abode of the mentally ill.

I am utterly powerless to describe the abject terror which seized me when I realized that I was within the four walls of a madhouse. Like the average man, my ignorance of institutional life was abysmal and profound. I simply catalogued them along with Dante's *Inferno* and let it go at that. They did not interest me.

In my earlier years, I once visited Ward's Island on some slumming expedition or the other. I remember being highly amused by one old lady whose sad plight should have claimed my tenderest sympathy, but did not move me. In the few moments I spent with her, out of morbid curiosity, she confided to me that she was the wife of Napoleon. In the next sentence her husbands changed to Henry Ward Beecher, Lincoln and Washington. "Won't you sit down?" I said, motioning to a chair. "No, thank you," she answered, "I am made of lead and if I sit down I will never be able to get up again."

I remember how my gay companions and myself had amused ourselves on the way home with anecdotes of this sort gleaned from the afternoon's experience. Now, in my own musing, it all flashed through my mind with the freshness and vividness of an event that I had just witnessed, and I felt a stab at the heart, as I recalled the utter callousness of my conduct on that sunny, carefree afternoon, now so many years ago. I could not help feeling that my present predicament was something in the nature of a just, though somewhat tardy, retribution.

My reveries were interrupted by the approach of an orderly who somewhat brusquely conducted me to the desk of the charge nurse, a courteous young man who I afterwards learned was the foreman, so to speak, of the section to which I had been assigned. This was where patients were kept the first few days after admission till their classification was determined. It is known technically as the Observation Ward, and here all cases are assembled pending the decision of the doctors regarding the exact nature of one's illness. During your stay in this ward you go through the necessary formula prescribed by all institutions. You sign a lot of papers, agreeing to abide by all the rules, of which at this time you know nothing and care less. The history of your case has accompanied your arrival. The doctors having read this, now examine you for a further diagnosis. It may be that your condition demands that you go to bed forthwith, to remain there till orders are received that you may get up. You are bathed, shaved, and arrayed in a pair of the hospital's artistic pajamas made of light yachting canvas, which resemble nothing so much as a short-skirted Mother Hubbard. Not a good-looking garment, but capable of much service, scrupulously clean and not at all uncomfortable. They are not, however, reminiscent of the natty silk suits of yesteryear.

After a while, an intern appears who inserts a sharp instrument at the base of your spine and extracts a small sample of your spinal fluid to be put into a tube labeled with your name and sent to the laboratory. Blood is also taken from the finger tips and from one or two of the arterial veins. The test of these blood samples reveals whether you have diabetes, skin troubles, Bright's disease, or are a general nuisance any way you look at it. These tests have to do with your body entirely; others, for your mental trouble, are a wholly separate function. A huge bell-shaped helmet closes over most of your head. I do not know what it registers, but it gives the doctors some idea of the disturbance within your "nut" which is the cause of your trouble.

Then there are the intelligence tests. You count small round balls on a frame and do simple sums in arithmetic. You are also asked to repeat a number of sentences. If you have no difficulty in meeting this test, you are then asked to try the same sentences backward. I think I averaged about 75, which thrilled me much. Afterwards, when I found out that everybody averaged "about 75," I wasn't so pleased. At all events, the doctors seemed satisfied. The blood tests revealed no organic complications, and physically I passed a fairly satisfactory examination. I was much underweight, had no appetite, and was extremely agitated. Sleep was an entire stranger and I paced the floor ceaselessly and vigorously. To sit down or stand still was an utter impossibility. To remedy this condition, I was sentenced to what is known as the Prolonged Bath Treatment. This is a bath constantly maintained at blood heat, 98 degrees, and the water continually renews itself. My body was rubbed with olive oil to prevent the skin from "puckering" (apt to result from long immersion if this precaution is omitted.) A heavy canvas cloth is stretched beneath the patient so that he does not rest on the hard substance of the stone bath itself, but on what is virtually a floating hammock. In addition to all this and across the tub, completely screening the body from view, is another canvas top, laced to the sides of the tub.

A nurse is detailed to watch the patient, a thermometer is frequently used to check the exact temperature of the water and a written record kept by the attendant of the patient's reaction to the treatment. These prolonged baths are given only on the signed order of the doctor in charge of that hall. He prescribes the time the bath should last and receives a written report of the operation and its conclusion. If no change is observable in the patient, at the expiration of the time prescribed for the bath, it may be lengthened in the judgment of the doctor. If that still continues ineffective, the "pack" is brought into play.

This consists of a series of ice-cold sheets wrapped around the patient one after another, till he resembles an Egyptian mummy. The shock of the ice-cold sheet after a hot bath has a therapeutic value very much the same as that a well man experiences when he plunges into the ocean on a hot summer day. The natural warmth of the body soon permeates the cold sheets. A heavy woolen blanket has meantime been wrapped around the sheets, which keeps the body heat intact. The effect of this treatment is to enervate the body without weakening it. I went though this gleeful experience, minus the cold pack, during the frigid months of July and August for two hours each morning and afternoon. It furnished opportunity for thought. I recalled the many delightful games of golf with which I was wont to beguile such summer days in the past, and these memories frequently induced me to say things not found in the Gospels. They also occasionally prevailed upon me to kick the covers off the tub, which caused the alarm bell to be sounded; whereupon all and sundry attendants would suddenly appear, to reinforce the rather nervous attendant who had me in charge. This young man had merely failed to appreciate my delight, while making an imaginary hole in one, at being cooped up in a hot tub with the outside temperature at 90 degrees. When the reason for the commotion was explained, the extra troops were withdrawn.

These baths lasted, I think, more than six months before the joyful order to discontinue was received. I did not think they did me any good. Still, without them, I might have tried to crawl on the ceiling or tip over the dining room table, just to hear the dishes rattle. You can never tell.

It is not an unusual occurrence for a badly disturbed patient to spend the whole day in one of these baths. That is a long time, and probably seems cruel to you, but I hardly think it is. He must be, by law, released every two hours for examination. During the time a patient is in this violent condition he is likely to hurt himself; or try to hurt someone else. In a bath, he is naturally under restraint, which is much better than running amuck among dozens of others. The safety and comfort of *all* is one of the main objects of the doctor's procedure, and a single patient cannot be allowed to set a whole ward aflame.

Another application of the water treatment is what is known as the "hydrobath." The Hydrobath Department was the only section not in keeping with the swagger standards prevailing elsewhere. It was evidently designed by some former patient—a gas fitter laboring under the delusion that he was an architect. He, no doubt, drew his ideas from Noah's Ark and not from the home of Aspasia. Be that as it may, this delightful contribution to the efficiency of modern psychiatry is in a class by itself. Presiding over it was a former Swiss papal guard, minus the picturesque costume of different colored trouser legs designed by Michelangelo, who also massaged our classic torsos, during such time as he was not occupied in the baths. His favorite war cries were: "The o-t-h-e-r s-i-d-e p-l-e-a-s-e," "T-u-r-n a-r-o-u-nd!" etc.

The hydro consists of hot and cold showers alternating, with a hose playing up and down your spine for variety. The sudden transition from hot to cold water is quite effective in startling you from any reverie into which you may have fallen; but beyond that I could see nothing in it.

Yet, curiously enough, I finally began to enjoy the experience and it ultimately produced a feeling of exhilaration as the cold water dashed over my body, and I felt the same tonic effect as I formerly did in the morning shower at home. You certainly couldn't take the change of the cold water right after the hot without bracing yourself for the shock, and this required considerable of that mental effort which I imagine the doctors were after. Some of these days, I presume we shall see huge swimming pools added to the equipment of hospitals just as in Y.M.C.A.'s. I suppose, though, a lot of the patrons of these pools will try to drown themselves, which would be something of a nuisance.

Twenty-five years ago the prolonged bath and the hydro were unknown. Their use is not even today as widely extended as it should be, but all the new hospitals are now being equipped with them. When the baths fail to calm the patient, they resort to the "camisole." This is a heavy canvas bag with openings for the arms and legs. It appears to be a poor relation of the sleeping bag sold by the swank sports shops. When the patient is thus encased, the bag is then laced up, leaving only an opening for the head. When it is desired to restrict movements entirely, the camisole containing the patient is laid in the bed and is laced to the iron frame of the bedstead. Feeding is done by injecting a soft gruel through a tube in the nose. To be encased in such a garment, perhaps for days at a time, is not a pleasant experience, but it is not nearly so painful nor so brutal as the hideous old mechanical wood and iron straitjacket, which it has supplanted.

That was an inheritance from inquisitorial days and seemed to possess the same evil spirit. Its use is now forbidden by law and it is some years since it disappeared completely from use in New York State Hospitals and I believe in others as well.

I remained in the Observation Ward a very long time. It was many weary weeks before the joyful news reached me that I could get up and dress. I had the freedom of the corridors, but an outdoor walk was as yet withheld.

My ward had a small "population" as they say in hospitals—there were less than thirty, though the number varied from day to day. Sometimes a quiet patient would suddenly become violent; so without any fuss and feathers he would be gently removed to the halls where disturbed patients lived, i.e., the wild ones. On the whole it was quite comfortable.

They never use the words "crazy" or "insane" in those hospitals. You are "depressed" or "disturbed" if you are quiet, or raising Hades, as the case may be. You are never "worse"; you are "not so well" today, but you are "getting better."

Apparently a great deal depends on language in mental cases. It is quite easy to increase depression by a slip of the tongue, and every nurse and attendant is carefully trained always to make an optimistic reply. Patients are continually discussing their condition and talk about their troubles incessantly, so all the doctors and nurses unite in saying: "You look better today," and "You are coming along nicely." This Pollyanna spirit was nauseating to me at first, but toward the end I could see its benefits. You may be sick—we all were—yet we were readily made worse by any remark that tended to reveal the true state of affairs and correspondingly encouraged when the doctors lied to us like gentlemen and said, "You look fine this morning." I never realized before the importance, the physical value, of optimism on the human mind. I am now fully convinced that it is of considerable specific therapeutic value.

Despite all attempts to encourage me, and the prolonged baths, I still continued to feel exactly as Dr. Johnson expressed himself in a situation precisely similar. A few days before his death the great lexicographer was very low and despondent.

"I have been as a dying man all night," he said, to Dr. Broklesly on his usual morning visit, and then, emphatically and almost unconsciously, broke out in these words of Shakespeare:

> "Canst though not minister to a mind diseased,
> Pluck from the memory a rooted sorrow,
> Raze out the written troubles of the brain,
> And with some sweet oblivious antidote,
> Cleanse the stuff'd bosom of that perilous stuff
> Which weighs upon the heart?"

To which the good doctor replied, and from the same poet:

> "Therein the patient
> Must minister to himself."

That is the great trouble in mental illness. You must pull yourself out of the hole. The doctor can do but little. All things pass away in this life, however, and to my great joy my detention in the Observation Ward finally came to an end. I was transferred to another in which the day's routine was more strenuous and included the blessing of once more being outdoors. My progress was slow. Personally, I could see no improvement. I resigned myself to my fate and gave way to settled melancholia. My reaction, however, should not reflect too adversely on the Hospital. They were doing all they could for me. I either could not, or would not, share their belief in my ultimate recovery which they constantly insisted was a physical certainty. That was hard for me to believe.

The Order of the Bath now being nothing but a memory, and my detention indoors ended, I was privileged to go outside part of the day. It felt good to breathe the fresh air and see the sky once more.

Chapter Three

I See and Hear Strange Things

Looking backward to my illness, I can now recall with more or less surprise my utter indifference to the beautiful environment which surrounded me on all sides in my Castle of Despair.

The Hospital was located in a naturally ideal situation. The buildings stood on the crest of a high hill, and the superb elevation commanded enchanting views in every direction. In the distance one saw the sparkling waters of Long Island Sound. A pretty little suburban town with its neat villas and charming houses nestled at the foot. Toward evening the slow disappearing sun would send a shaft of gold against the burnished towers of the skyscrapers of New York. English ivy, not an easy plant to grow in this country, covered the walls of the buildings completely. It started to climb them more than half a century ago and now reaches the eaves, sheltering a myriad of feathered friends in its ascent. The royal oaks and sycamores; the rare, decorative shrubs and dwarf trees brought from all over the world; the gorgeous rhododendrons, hydrangeas, rose bushes and geraniums, bordering the walks; the magnificent box hedges that separated one field from another, and the Norway spruce and pine trees of rare silver coloring that dotted the lawns at intervals, sounded a pleasing note.

All this beauty was lost on me. Yet is must have had a soothing effect upon the subconscious mind and perhaps brought healing in its wings all unknown to me.

I have since revisited the scene of my drama several times and I always sneak off to what I called Sunset Hill, for that gorgeous evening view. That I many times stood on exactly the same spot and saw nothing, remains to me one of the mysteries of that strange interlude; but as a matter of fact, had I stood there with an atrociously aching tooth, I don't think I would have seen anything either. The mind was sick and ached instead of a tooth, and that was all there was to it.

I do recall that gradually I began to anticipate those sunsets and to wait impatiently for the starling and blackbirds to return to the trees. We had thousands of them. It was a sanctuary for them, and they seemed to know it was a harbor of refuge and a place of peace, which indeed it was—for more than the birds. This aroused interest was a sign of returning health, but to me it meant absolutely nothing, I was now a "nut," and I would never be well again—Never! Never! Never!

Our Hospital, as I have just stated, had very beautiful grounds and very pleasing prospects, but the buildings were old. Many of our State Hospitals were erected coincident with the fall of the Roman Empire—particularly the one on Ward's Island. Those that date only from the Christian Era are called "new."

The one I was in belonged to the latter period, and in my particular ward we had swinging wooden doors leading to the bathrooms. All day long these doors would give a good imitation of machine gun fire with their incessant tat-tat-tatting.

Then that prehistoric device for locating doctors was in full flower—the fire-alarm gong. No matter how drowsy you were, or how much you wished to be quiet, these strident gongs would ring incessantly in a vain attempt to find a doctor who was somewhere among the twenty-odd wards. We also rejoiced in a magnificently endowed trans-Atlantic steam whistle which not only woke the living, but all the dead for miles around. This was to let you know that it was 7 a.m.

Some doctor recently, during a lucid interval, installed electric lights in the rooms and dormitories of one hospital. Promptly at the rising hour these lights suddenly came on and had the same soothing effect as if you had turned on a loud speaker. I ought not to mention loud speakers. They might substitute them for the gongs.

Most of the doctors' private offices had an air of sanctuary about them. This was largely due to the dim religious lights pervading them and not, as you may have imagined, to the saintly conduct of their occupants. Many padded cells have better light than some doctors' offices.

The doctors come around every morning and give each patient a genial greeting, a quick and searching glance. An assistant accompanies each doctor to take notes of any complaints or requests. He usually stands close at the back of the doctor. This is a mark of deference. It is also to ward off any playful familiarities that may be offered the good medico, such as sticking a knife in his back, or crowning him with a heavy water pitcher. The former occurrence took place not long ago in another hospital and the grapevine telegraph promptly brought us the news. It is all in the day's work.

Now this cheerfulness in the morning's greeting has a distinct therapeutic value. If a doctor appeared with an unmistakable grouch and was plainly down in the mouth, it would have its immediate reaction on the patient. When he smiled and gave a hearty, "Good morning, gentlemen, fine morning, isn't it? Typical Westchester weather." You felt better than if he mumbled under his breath that the day was fine. The patients accordingly responded in like manner, lying like gentlemen when they said they felt fine. All but me; I'd remark that I felt like hell and was worse than ever. I was what they called the doctors' ducky darling boy. That the doctors' smiles were manufactured fresh every morning in the Hospital's own laboratory and issued to all the doctors in common, did not, in my estimation, impair either their usefulness, or effectiveness. They prided themselves on the quality of their laboratory products and to do them justice, I think they were entitled to all they claimed. I often tried to detect the places where the smile was welded to the face, but never was able to discover the joints. It was a very fine piece of work.

On the whole, however, the new ward was not at all bad. The group with whom I found myself was not so "sick"; in other words, not so balmy as in the Observation Ward. I began to look around, to pick out those I thought I would like best to associate with and to take account of stock generally. "The proper study of mankind is man," I quoted myself, and I proceeded to arrange my plans accordingly.

The inside of a Cuckoo Mansion proved a most excellent place in which to pursue these philosophic reflections. There are probably more, and possibly better, specimens of the *genus homo* outside, but they are not classified, labeled and enclosed in glass boxes, as they are in a hospital; and the collection is fairly representative; the variety embraces practically every known species. On the whole, it may be said to be quite a comprehensive group and not merely the flotsam and jetsam of a turbulent tide.

We had some really distinguished guests—General Pershing, Napoleon, Field Marshal Foch, Herbert Hoover, Mussolini, Ramsay MacDonald, "John D.," Mayor Walker and Henry Ford. On the women's side there were the Queen of Sheba, Mary Pickford, Greta Garbo, Ethel Barrymore, Katharine Cornell, Lady Astor, Fannie Hurst and Edna Ferber. We did not lack for brilliant people and my study of their personalities proved diverting and interesting.

I accordingly picked out one or two that I decided might perhaps prove more congenial than the rest. There are some queer fish in a State Hospital and even under such weird circumstances one still retains one's likes and dislikes. It was tacitly understood that all such friendships were temporary and were not to be continued outside the castle walls. There was one young patient, under his thirties I should imagine, for whom I conceived a special liking. His temporary trouble was that he didn't know what it was all about. He was tall, straight as an arrow, and good looking. He had one of the most charming personalities it has ever been my good fortune to meet. He was, at the same time, possibly the most romantic and most magnificent liar that ever graced our terrestrial globe.

His story, as he told it to me, had its beginning on the Somme at the Great Offensive. He was a Canadian, and one day he showed me, in a moment of sacred confidence, a small bronze medal which I immediately recognized as the Victoria Cross. He ventured no remarks concerning it, and although I was consumed with curiosity, I suppressed, with great difficulty, a multitude of questions that surged to my lips. In time I got the whole story, but weeks would intervene between one chapter and the next.

On the night of this engagement in the War he was separated from the rest of his command and taken prisoner. In the confusion of the German retreat the next day, he wandered off and his mind became a blank. He recalls that while walking through a picturesque, little, French village, he was suddenly stopped by a young woman who threw her arms around his neck and covered his face with kisses. The woman led him to a house, weeping and laughing at the same time. "Here he is—safe and sound!" she cried to several people who appeared in the doorway, "I knew he would come back,"and impulsively she threw her arms around him before everybody.

It was apparently a case of mistaken identity. At the time, he was unable to talk much or even think clearly. It was plain to be seen that he was utterly exhausted. He was only too glad to be led to a chamber and to suffer his clothes to be removed by his newly found wife. He slept all that afternoon and night, to awake the next morning ravenously hungry..

"I remember the whole scene distinctly," he said, as we sat on a bench one afternoon, "but what the woman's name was, or the town, I cannot for the life of me recall, nor how long I stayed there. It must have been many months, possibly years. I do not know. I remember that it was very beautiful, and that the woman was very kind to me, and there was a little baby. I can still feel her little warm body in my arms. Her eyes were the color of mine. I was very happy, only I could not understand it. I seemed to be another person.

"I could not recall many things, which to my wife seemed sacrilege, and it was. The anniversary of our wedding—her birthday—our honeymoon on the Mediterranean. It was dastardly of me to forget them, of course. 'You must pardon me,' I would say in an agony of remorse, when I noticed the pain on her face, 'but that night in No Man's Land—it blotted out many things.' Her answer to this was an affectionate embrace and many kisses. 'Forgive me,' she would say, 'I did not mean to hurt you.'

"That's what she got for having a gorilla around the house," he added sorrowfully.

"I was seated alone one morning in a rose bower overlooking our lake. The Curé of the village entered. 'And are you well and happy this morning?' he said, taking a seat beside me and placing his hand gently on my shoulder.

" 'Yes, my good friend. Very happy. Very contented.'

" 'A great surgeon is coming to see you this morning from Vienna.'

" 'So?'

" 'Yes. You will see him?'

"At this moment, the woman entered. There were tear stains on her face and I knew she had been weeping. 'He thinks he can cure you, Paul, and I think so too, but you must go away for awhile.'

" 'Is that why you are crying? You needn't. I will gladly suffer anything for you. What is the matter with me? I feel all right.'

" 'But you cannot remember. You do not always know that you are my dear husband. You do not sometimes know your little Jean. It was *that* night.'

"After that," he said, rising suddenly, "everything is blank. I was brought here, they tell me, from a cellar where I had been found in New York. Who am I anyhow?"

And he moved off.

That was a severe case of amnesia. How much of his story was true, I do not know. He was found in a cellar, as he stated, and the police traced his movements back to his home in Montreal, which he had left six months before. He had returned there from somewhere in France several years after the War. Where, no one knew, and he had forgotten.

I found myself constructing quite a romance out of this story that afternoon. It afforded me much needed mental occupation. It drove my own black thoughts out of my head completely for the time being and I was more and more convinced that my sky piece was improving, or it could never have retained this story and dwelt upon it as it was doing.

This gradual awakening of the brain was to me an absorbing panorama. I followed it with ever-growing interest. To me it seemed like a play. When the curtain descended, all was blank. When it rose again, the action moved on as if no interruption had occurred, and I followed out this simile to its logical conclusion. This hospital play would end eventually, but life would go on just as it does after we leave the theater.

Seated on the same bench another afternoon, my neighbor quietly handed me a telegram which had just come in. The message was to the effect that his company would expend twenty millions on betterments to care for their expanding business. This chap's real job was to be Chairman of the Board, but he preferred the more diverting, though less eminent, part of clown. "If they keep on," he remarked, looking at the telegram, "I'll have hard work to raise the price of a frail when I get out." Only that and nothing more. He has since shot himself.

Some patients took a savage delight occasionally in raising a deliberate rumpus. I met one of them who was taking a stroll guarded by two attendants. He was a young college student and a splendid fellow. He showed marks of having been through the mill. "It took seven of 'em to hold me," he cried out gleefully as we passed each other, "and two of 'em are still listening to the birdies."

His was an exhilaration case. I forget the medical term for it, but it's the reverse of depression. In the exuberance of his spirits, the fine young boy—only nineteen—wanted to "show off." He had made the varsity team in baseball and football, and was on his way toward acquiring new laurels as a member of the crew, when he exploded. In a few weeks, I am happy to state, his nerves gradually quieted down and he was able to rejoin his class after only about three months' absence. I shall never forget how well he looked the day he left and how glad I was to see him go.

Another case that I recall was that of a very husky-looking chap, a prototype of the stage Irishman of Harrigan and Hart days, who rather intrigued me. In knee breeches, long-tailed coat, high hat, and a clay pipe, he could have made a first-rate Celtic comedian. Comedians are always morose and bad-tempered offstage, and this Bejabbers person ran true to type. If I remarked, "This is a fine morning; how's every little thing with you?" He would answer, "Mind your own business. I didn't speak to you," and move off in another direction. That's what they call a paranoiac in cuckoo land. Outside we call them grouches.

I finally was at considerable pains to let this gentleman know my real feelings toward him. In my innocent Japanese way, I called to him across the campus, "You big bum, why don't you go home and go to work? There's nothing the matter with you but laziness and you know it." Not having asbestos on which to write, I am unable to preserve his answer to posterity.

I was also at great pains to point out to a somewhat elderly patient, who had married a young and very pretty wife, the vast benefits which would accrue to her in the event of his sad demise. He had a hundred thousand dollar policy, with no anti-suicide clause. So I enlarged upon the eternal gratitude in which she would always hold his memory if he would kindly bump himself off. Delicate attentions like this did much to enhance my popularity.

Generally speaking, there are two classes in all hospitals. Those who can talk and those who can't or won't. One of them I met at this time hadn't spoken a word for nearly five years. The "Delusioners," as we called them, are those who constantly saw things or heard voices and were more talkative. I much prefer them.

So the discourses of the Delusioners were to me a welcome relief from the gloom and silence of the "Depressives." I found myself becoming more interested daily. It was a little uncanny, of course, to hear "Napoleon" again recall the night before Austerlitz. As I turned to leave him, he posed as if standing on the deck of the *Bellerophon*. "My dear Marshal," he said, toying with his forelock and lapsing into French, "*Nous cou-cherons ce soir à Bruxelles.*" At this reference to Waterloo, a vision of St. Helena rose in the distance.

Or to hear "Antony" again give voice to his anguish at the death of Caesar. To my really serious and honest inquiry, "Why did Anthony and Caesar both fall in love with Cleopatra?" I received no answer. A sixteen-year-old girl who could turn the heads of two conquerors of the world, had always appealed to me, and I was genuinely interested in seeking to know if this mind of ours, unleashed from earthly bondage, would glimpse aught else than was vouchsafed the normal sons of men.

"Mussolini" was quite interesting, though voluble. "Why," said I, "do you call Liberty a putrescent corpse?"

"Because liberty is leisure and you have no leisure. Your government elects one man to administer justice and a hundred to prevent him from doing it. Meanwhile Jimmy Gerard's Sixty-four Immortals are sucking our life's blood. Your national bird is not an eagle; it's a buzzard. Bah!"

There were times when these conversations changed from inanity to irritation.

At the conclusion of a golf game, I asked one of our foursome what his score was. "You will have to see my doctor. I do not care to discuss the matter with any patient." This used to make me ill. Not the stupidity or the gross discourtesy, but the knowledge driven home inescapably, that you were in the land of phantasmagoria.

On the whole, I think I enjoyed "General Foch" as much as any one. Not for the profoundness of his philosophy or the depth of his erudition, but because of his all-around efficiency. He commanded the Anzacs at Gallipoli and single-handedly massacred all the Turks on the Peninsula. He captured Jerusalem, but generously allowed Allenby the credit and (confidentially) was the Mysterious Flying Apparition of the Arabian Desert—Capt. Lawrence. These were only his minor accomplishments. His real life was spent as Chief Justice of the Supreme Court, Sergeant of Marines and house detective of the old Waldorf. He was also lecturer, traveler, scientist, and author of several books—*Adam Bede*, *Dombey and Son* and *Alice in Wonderland*. To talk with him after the vapid utterances of the Irish comedian and the golf champion was a relief. It was, of course, rather trying to have him always assume the attitude of a Roman senator addressing the Tribune, which he invariably did when fairly well launched on one of his orations; but the variety of his conferences, the multifarious roles which he had filled during his former existence, furnished a welcome interlude to the monotony of the endless days. One was quite exhausted after a session, to be sure; but he whiled the time away, and to this extent was a public benefactor of no small proportions.

There was another military genius, "General Pershing," who had a golf suit with riding boots and a slouch hat that made him able to impersonate a US Army general to perfection. He carried field glasses strung across his shoulders and walked with martial tread. He had some idea of military life, because he showed me how a camp should be pitched on high ground near water and the sanitary arrangements located so that drainage would seep away from, and not into, the camp. When the squads lined up for morning exercises, he always took a place at the head of the column and carefully inspected the men from the rear. At the conclusion of his self-imposed task, he would take two paces to the front, click his heels and march, arms touching his trousers, up to the physical instructor. "I have the honor to report, sir, all present and accounted for." Then he would salute, again turn on his heel and resume observation of the field through his binoculars. He liked playing soldier, but I imagine his real job of peddling sham silk hosiery from door to door rather took the romance out of his life.

>>>>>>>>>>>>>>> Chapter Four <<<<<<<<<<<<<<

"You Will Get Well!"

About this time I remember meeting the celebrated Professor Bleuler one afternoon, direct from his Psychiatric Institute in Zürich, probably the most famous on the Continent. The best of them all however is right here in our own country. It cured me. But, no man is a hero to his own valet. Professor Bleuler was here to attend a Mental Hygiene Congress convened under the direction of Clifford W. Beers, whose amazing experience in our State Hospitals thirty years ago led him to attack the ignorance and abuses then prevalent in the treatment of the insane. His book, *A Mind That Found Itself*, resulted in the organization of the movement now so general throughout the United States, operating as Mental Hygiene Committees. Mr. Beers has done a wonderful work, and the improved methods of care and treatment are largely due to his unceasing efforts in this direction.

A son of Professor Bleuler had me for a "specimen" while he was studying in our Hospital, and my antics and repercussions doubtless both puzzled and amused him. At all events, he was sufficiently interested in his "experiments" to draw his famous father's attention to the strange and singular being upon whom he was working.

Aside from the fact that the good professor has an unusually well-shaped forehead and bears unmistakably the marks of a genuine scientist, he would be dismissed physically as not being particularly striking. He is the inventor, however, of that term in psychiatry known as "Schizophrenia," which means a cleavage or division of the mind. Such a person is portrayed in Stevenson's famous romance *Dr. Jekyll and Mr. Hyde.*

Professor Bleuler has changed this fiction into reality. There were several cases in our Hospital. The one that interested me most was that of a young man who was also ambidextrous and an artist of considerable ability. With his left hand he drew the most beautiful picture imaginable; and they were delightful in their power and beauty. With his right hand, however, he let loose the dregs of hell. The fiendish shapes, the grotesque figures, the naked bestiality of his drawings were revolting. It was hard to conceive of such human degradation.

His case to me was of absorbing interest. I would have given a good deal to have been transferred to his ward where I could have seen him more frequently and studied him at leisure. His conversation, such little as I was enabled to hear, was apparently governed by the same peculiar cleavage. During the short talks I had with him, his conversation was perfectly intelligent and rational. We discussed natural history. Since I had mentioned my connection with the Museum of the City of New York, he confused it with museums relating to birds, beasts, and other natural history subjects in which he was particularly interested. He was quite able to understand the difference between a historical museum and the other kind, and I subsequently procured for him some catalogs from Dr. Osborne, which pleased him very much.

Of course, this dual personality was the source of constant trouble. He would be discussing the habits of lions, tigers, whales and such, when suddenly voices would command him to punch you on the nose; and unless you were on the alert, such a catastrophe was quite apt to happen. He could not, under these circumstances, be allowed much freedom. It was awkward, to say the least, to be always on the lookout for that fist, nor could you judge in advance, with any degree of accuracy, just when it would suddenly start out in the direction of your eye. Consequently, conversation with him always involved considerable nervous strain. There were, however, frequent periods when this destructive urge was entirely absent. The doctors predicted that as deterioration progressed, this feature of his illness would subside. In due time it would disappear entirely, because the deterioration would have progressed so far that the unhappy victim would have become a *corpus delicti*.

But this curious phenomenon of a glowing and heavenly side to his nature, existing contemporaneously with the sinister spirits of evil, held me transfixed. It produced a curious and fascinating appeal which was hard to ignore. I gave him, however, a high rating in the list of things that I thought started my own befuddled brain on the upward path, because he made me think, and when you begin to think, you have made a start on the road to recovery.

There was one other thing about the visit of Professor Bleuler which I can recall with gratitude and thankfulness. After giving me a searching inspection, he turned to his son and said, "This man will get well." Holding out his hand, he added, "Good night, my friend, no matter what you think, you will get well." It is this doctor who diagnosed Nijinsky's case and pronounced him incurable.

I managed to conjure up a few choice but emphatic maledictions which I was about to hurl at this head, when the door closed and he had disappeared up the corridor.

Quite a number of patients were in our Hospital as a result of business troubles. Wall Street supplied the majority, of course, but there were some whose reverses were legitimate. For example, a manufacturer was sent to the wall by a rival's development of a new process which had been offered to him first, but which he had declined. Then there were others whose errors in judgment caused them to fail. There was one for whom I had little or no sympathy.

When I first knew him, he was a clerk in a very small retail store. I doubt if his income was much over twelve hundred dollars a year. Just before the crash, he was offered two hundred million dollars for his various properties, which he refused. Visions of eclipsing Rockefeller, Carnegie and a lot of others were in his brain. So today he is in a sanitarium. During his stay with us, certain Court proceedings disclosed the fact that he had practically nothing left. I never did like a hog.

His was a clear case of "Superiority Complex," as the doctors call it. One of the doctors told me that a good many successful business men suffer from this complaint, and in every instance it indicates a mental flaw in an otherwise admirable structure. "Few men," he continued, "can fairly claim to be sole architects of their own careers. Fortunate circumstances, accidental opportunities, exceptional happenings of one kind or another are present in every case of success. Yet we must grant them the credit of having seized their opportunities. Without these extraordinary happenings they might have worked just as hard, just as intelligently, with no particular result. For that reason, humility and a recognition of the kindness of the Gods should be a part of every man's make-up.

"This frame of mind will always keep him on even keel. The successful man is always surrounded by sycophants and flatterers. He can't escape them nor their baleful influence. He must struggle against them constantly. Otherwise, they run a good chance of being left naked in their old age in the presence of their enemies.

"This is after all a mental disease, but one so insidious as to be difficult of recognition. It needs a good strong background to stand the strain of unusual success, and in the case of many self-made men, this background is lacking. Every one of us can well afford to spend a quiet hour occasionally taking stock of ourselves and giving credit for success to the thousand and one circumstances that have helped make us what we are and not appropriate the whole credit to ourselves. This would have kept the ambition of this patient within reasonable bounds and from thinking that his was the only brain that had operated to achieve success."

Other men are today in a similar position, and if they will only stop and weigh all the circumstances of their rise, carefully and thoughtfully, they may be halted in some additional undertaking, that lacks the happy combination which existed in the original success. Men rarely venture into another and unknown business successfully, solely because they have succeeded in one which they know all about. This Superiority Complex is hard to handle and is greatly complicated by the army of "yes men" with whom the victim is invariably surrounded. John D. Rockefeller, Sr. seems to be conspicuous among the men I recall who would listen to his associates. It frequently happened that he was compelled to yield to their combined judgment. That he was able to do so showed his real greatness. You may be sure that it was not without great effort that he did so. "He who conquereth his own spirit is greater than he that taketh a city."

I knew another very successful man who built a huge mansion. The Civil War ruined him and the great house fell into the hands of Governor Samuel J. Tilden who in turn passed it along to its present owner, another equally distinguished citizen and famous member of the Bar, Samuel Untermyer.

After the war the original owner and builder of this great house—Greystone—recovered his fortune.

He wanted his happiness to continue, so he made no effort to regain possession of his former great estate. He contented himself with a modest cottage, smaller than the lodge house of Greystone, and there he spent the evening of his life in peace and contentment.

This tale is not told to illustrate that pride goeth before a fall, but to call attention to a prolific source of mental trouble—greed and overweening ambition. These two worthy souls work night and day for insane asylums and sanitariums and never ask remuneration for their services. Their clients, however, pay dearly.

Our physicians insisted that you can forget your troubles, and they are right. It's hard, but by no means impossible. I made mistakes and serious ones. If I were to stop and think of the past it would only be a very short time before I would be back in the old padded cell again. So when I tell a man or a woman that recovery is in their own hands, I am not telling them something I have read in a book, or repeating what some doctor has told me. I am talking from actual personal experience.

Some mourn at shattered Fortune's bier,
In darkened room bewail their dead—
But others hail in vision clear,
The promise of the day ahead!

There is absolutely no sense in bewailing the past. That slogan is constantly heard in all hospitals, and I knew one of the doctors to admit that every time he thinks of certain lines of Shakespeare he almost goes mad himself. "They belong," he said, "in the same category with that biblical fable, which tells us that work is a curse and was sent as a punishment for the sins of Adam and Eve. As a matter of fact, work is God's best gift to man. Shakespeare's brilliant contribution to the world's best line of "hooey" is this:

There is a tide in the affairs of men,
Which, taken at the flood, leads on to fortune;
Omitted, all the voyage of their life
Is bound in shallows and in miseries.

"If I wanted to keep a lot of depressed men forever depressed," he said, "I would have them recite that beautiful thought daily, along with morning prayers; but if I wanted to talk sympathetically to get them well, I would prove by unimpeachable evidence that this statement is absolutely wrong. I could cite them innumerable instances where men had triumphed again and again over a first mistake. I would also turn to another gifted genius who may not be so widely known as Shakespeare, but in one instance, at least, had much better sense than the great Bard of Avon. This comparatively unknown poet, Walter Malone, handles the same idea in this lovely and heartwarming fashion:

"They do me wrong who say I come no more
When once I knock and fail to find you in;
For every day I stand outside your door
And bid you wake, and rise to fight and win.

Wail not for precious chances passed away!
Weep not for golden ages on the wane!
Each night I burn the records of the day—
Each sunrise every soul is born again!"

The feat that haunts a man who has suddenly become poor, is that he must go to work again, and this biblical fable about work being a curse is about the worst thing he can get into his head. If he thinks work is a curse, let him be shut up in an insane asylum for a few years, and be physically able to work but absolutely powerless to do so, and he will discover what is a *real* curse. Work is a perfectly normal, healthful, attribute of life.

Mankind can no more live without work than he can without breathing, and one is just as natural as the other. Take away work, or the power to work, and you have accomplished a real tragedy. The ability that enabled him to build up a fortune in the first place is still his exclusive property and as good as ever. Therefore, why worry?

We all cheerfully admit that money cannot buy everything, and the things it cannot buy are invariably the worthwhile things.

If that is true, then money cannot be such a priceless possession as it is thought to be. So why blow your brains out because you have lost a little of something that is not so tremendously important after all? There is absolutely no virtue in repining. There is positive harm and real danger in thinking back to what might have been. In that direction lies only further depression and increased mental disturbance. I know it is hard to forget—no one knows better—no one know the pangs of a wasted life better, and I could think myself back into another period of illness without half trying, if I allowed my mind to dwell on these things. There's always another chance.

We are fashioned by nature to forget sorrow, anguish, and disappointment. When they are on us, we say to ourselves, "I'll never get over this. I'll never forget this to my dying day." It's not true. We all know it's not true of others and yet, incorrigible and hopelessly illogical, we doubt in ourselves the power to forget. We are even ashamed of forgetting.

That is silly. To pride one's self on the ability to suffer agonies over a past tragedy is idiotic.

Life is sweeping us through new and changing experiences. We change daily, hourly, moment by moment, and man forgets what is past whether he wants to or not.

Indeed, the power to forget is in exact proportion to the intensity of the bitterness. Take it for a fact, since it is one, that the more disagreeable your present, the more completely it will vanish. If you are desperate today, you can be absolutely certain that on some tomorrow, not long distant, you'll have clean forgotten what you were desperate about.

When some great sorrow, like a mighty river,
Flows through your life with peace-destroying power
And dearest things are swept from sight forever,
Say to your heart each trying hour'
This, too, will pass away.

As a matter of fact, lots of men make and lose several fortunes in a lifetime. No man ought ever to give up till the sod closes over him, and then he should make ready for the other life that is to come. Ninety percent of the cure is in forgetting the mistake that landed you where you are—in getting rid of the frightfully depressing thoughts that made you want to kill yourself most of the time.

In our Hospital those who possessed an ungovernable temper and refused to control it, did not find the going easy. When you broke out into one of your old-time tantrums, nobody excused you or sympathized with you. You were simply classed as non-cooperative and clapped into a cold pack or made into what is known in asylum colloquialism as an "ice cream sandwich." At all events, the outburst of your abnormal self, or whatever other fancy name you chose to give it, was effectually squelched by the application of this treatment, and it was astounding how quickly you became sweet-tempered and amiable as a result. If that drastic treatment had been administered to you in former years, your asylum experience need never have occurred. By your puerile self-excusing, by your lack of moral courage in facing a failing that your own common sense told you was silly and cruel, you preferred to ignore what was crying our for correction and quieted you conscience by the weak and stupid argument that "you couldn't help it," and prepared yourself for the asylum.

After a man has enjoyed the soothing effects of a cold pack, he discovers that a bad temper *can* be controlled if he puts forth the proper effort, and he spends quite a few days in vain regrets that he did not realize this sooner. I will not say that the fear of repetition of the cold pack is all that is at the bottom of this altered view, but I do say it has a great influence.

In the case of mature persons, it sometimes happens that an older man feels that he has earned the right to be as crotchety as he pleases. Particularly is this true of the man who has accomplished something and has reached a position of independence. He may have reached the latter stage in a financial sense, but at no time has he reached the other. The fact that he can afford to indulge himself is a mistaken idea. Not if he wishes to keep on living and enjoying life for a few more years. His arteries are more brittle. The old heart that carried him to the success which is his, cannot endure the strain it once did. No man reaches the top without a struggle, which cannot even be imagined by the young fellow starting out. It was no child's play and any man who has achieved a great position by his own efforts has paid for it both physically and mentally. Now let him enjoy his reward. Let him not burst an artery or send his blood pressure up by an unseemly display of temper. He has arrived. The day of storm and tempest is over. He is safely anchored in a haven of rest. Why not stay there a while and admire the works of God that may have heretofore been a closed book to him? The Spring with all Nature coming to life again. The Summer with its call outdoors; the Autumn with its alluring Indian Summer, and the Winter with its intellectual pleasures. Why leave all that you have fought for, struggled for, and now have in abundance? Stay here while you can. Avoid passionate outbursts as you would a plague.

A bad-tempered man knows his conduct is dastardly and breeds mischief and misery. When his passion is over, he is usually remorsefully repentant, but the evil he has done remains. The pain he has inflicted cannot easily be forgotten.

Now self-control is not an easy matter. Today I can control myself, but who wants to go through what I did to learn a lesson that can be acquired without all that hideous torment and suffering? I often think a few weeks spent in an insane asylum would be the greatest panacea for bad temper that could be devised. And there you would see a beautifully large proportion of men and women who owed their predicament to their charming habit of disregarding other people's rights and feelings whenever it pleased them so to do. Having your own way in this world is, I will admit, a fascinating pastime; but at the same time it is one of the most expensive forms of amusement of which I have any knowledge.

When day succeeds day and month succeeds month, with nothing to do and nothing to think about, when you are even sick of cussing the doctors, the attendants, the nurses, the institution and everything connected with the infernal outfit, you begin to wonder what to do next. To get up in the morning with a lot of things to do is bad enough; but to get up with nothing ahead of you but a long stretch of emptiness, is simply maddening. I resorted to all sorts of expedients to kill time except, of course, those things that the Hospital wanted me to do, which I thought was altogether too much of them to expect. So I would pick out here and there, at odd times, one or two patients less objectionable (if that were possible) to the general run and get them talking. As a rule, there was not much nourishment in this, but it was the best the larder afforded.

Occasionally the young nurses yielded better results. We had some rather pretty ones on our side for brief periods. They were student nurses taking their final studies which included a little practical experience in actual service. They stayed only a few weeks, and to them it was a novel and rather enjoyable experience. They had read a lot in their textbooks about neurosis and psychosis, and here they were to experience the delights of meeting these famous characters in person. I don't suppose anything in their whole course of training ever gave these sweet young things such a thrill as they experienced when actually placed in charge of a group of real "goofs."

The main point about talking to these charming young persons was that you could be sillier than if you were at a real society function and all your asinine remarks were accepted without question as part of your "balminess." "Would you like to see me crawl up the wall and walk across the ceiling?" I would ask of one of them, and she would politely say, "Yes, that would be very exciting, but not now please. It's time for your eggnog," or some equally clever answer. I used to enjoy the slight shock these questions gave them and racked my brain for all the fool things I could think of. I knew they would write home about their wonderful experience, and I tried to be good copy.

All of these little asides were, of course, of exceedingly short durations, and I felt the need of more substantial food for cogitation. Besides that, another thing was beginning to alarm me seriously. I began to fear the doctors were right after all and that soon I would be well again. At first I gave that suggestion short shrift, but I noticed that it appeared with increasing frequency. To my great relief it gradually began to lose its fearsomeness. It is not unusual for a patient to become "hospitalized," i.e., he becomes so accustomed to life without effort that he loses the ambition to face the complexities of life in the outside world. I accordingly began to prepare for a new entrance into life. Realizing that it had been a unique experience, I concluded to make notes of all that went on around me, especially those unconsidered trifles—opinions, theories, etc., of nurses, visitors, doctors, etc., that were dropped within ear-shot all the time. Some of them struck me as decidedly novel and well worth preserving. Everybody has his own idea of what's the best way to prevent nervous breakdowns and how you should conduct yourself so as to avoid such a catastrophe, but they are academical. Here was the chance to record the result of practical experience, and it should undoubtedly be of great value.

A great majority of these semi-professional opinions inclined to the belief that this illness was largely the patient's own fault; a conclusion which I had already reached, based on what I had seen myself for three years. So I am going to put in a few of these gleanings wherever I think they will serve to point a moral or adorn a tale.

I quickly found that it did me good to study the problem, and it helped me considerably in my fight toward normality. In addition to my study, as I called it, I did a lot of miscellaneous reading and was soon deep in Behaviorism, Mother Love, Alcoholism, Dementia Praecox, Schizophrenia, Maniacal Depression, and all the other neuroses and psychoses which form the stock in trade of hospital conversation. I would clip an item out of a paper or a psychiatric report of some kind and ask questions about it from the one I thought best qualified to answer. I was not interested from the medical side—only from the social, so to speak. I wanted to know what would keep a well person *well*; the sick people I would leave for the doctor. Many items in the papers on mental hygiene, though coming from authoritative sources, struck me as being rather queer, to say the least. So I thought I would make a note of those that appealed to me as rather unusual and bring them up for discussion at an opportune time. I gathered some rather interesting data that is not usually found in printed books. It is what they call "source material," I imagine, as it came from the first-hand experience of the people around me, who had worked among patients for years, and who had some rather excellent ideas of their own concerning cause and effect in mental cases. They are strictly non-medical, non-professional—just ordinary deductions based on this continuous contact with the nervously ill and I think have much value. They are at the bottom of whatever is valuable in this book.

Science works in such mysterious ways its wonders to perform that it is not right to laugh, as I did at first, at every item that seemed to me ridiculous. So many marvelous things have been developed from these crazy stunts, as I called them, that I no longer indulge in my former unrestrained merriment. To illustrate this point, let me give you this instance.

A writer in one of our prominent journals, more or less scientific, has worked out the theory that if mothers no longer love their children, the trouble is pathological. They just need a little more manganese in their diet, he claims. The theory has been tried out on rats. A number of rodents that displayed a lack of interest in their young were given a shot of manganese and at once lavished affection on their offspring. So, if Johnny has fallen through the ice, and has stayed out an hour or so in his wet clothes, your affection may temporarily lapse. In which event, before you tan Johnny, take a dose of manganese.

When I first read this, I thought I had a relapse and was sicker than ever. I showed the item to our doctor and he said I needn't be alarmed, I was quite all right. The doctors have seen so many marvels come out of the laboratory that nothing new surprises them; so they are now noncommittal. At all events, rats at present are certainly having a hard time with psychologists. They make them walk over hot irons to find out how strong certain instincts are in them. They are kept hungry or eager to meet their mate, or their curiosity is aroused in some way or other over these two emotions, and it is the frequency with which they will essay this painful journey that determines the strength of these instincts and reveals also the state of their neurosis, but what all this has to do with mother love is beyond me. Still it is one of the items that interested me, so I clipped it for reference. Other illustrations seemed just as far removed from psychiatry as this specimen, and yet in some way or other they are apparently closely related.

For those who read these pages and have loved ones incarcerated in these hospitals, I can only say that they need not look upon the situation as one of intolerable misery. One cannot, of course, expect better care than one would receive at home. That is hardly to be expected.

I do not, of course, mean to say that any of them are ideal places of residence. In fact, I have heard some men emphatically express a preference for a wooden box six feet underground. That, however, is a matter of individual taste. I will frankly admit that they are not Utopias. Nor will I claim that all the attendants are graduates of Harvard or Yale, nor have they given much study to the letters of Lord Chesterfield to his son.

No doubt there are many other places where you would much prefer to have your dear ones. That we will readily admit, but when they are afflicted with mental illness, they need to be isolated for a short time for the good of all concerned, and you must bear in mind that the State can never take the place of the family at any time—in sickness or in health. However, it does no good to worry. They may get into a little trouble at first because they are unused to the life that now confronts them. It is somewhat strange to be ordered about and told to do this and do that, but that must be faced. When a patient sees that a certain routine is absolutely essential under the circumstances and tries to be obedient and cooperative, he soon finds that it is much the better way. Hospitals haven't time to explain the reason for this and that order, any more than the Army has. Matters must move quickly and on schedule. A refractory patient can cause no end of confusion and interrupt the smooth running of the entire machinery. A moment's reflection will convince you that such conduct cannot possibly be tolerated. Some of the hospitals have between four and seven thousand patients. It is no small task to keep them occupied and make them comfortable. It is bad enough to handle that many persons under normal conditions, but when they are all highly nervous, easily excited by the most trivial happening, you can readily understand that the staff responsible for the management of the hospital has no slight task. It cannot be denied that there are instances of cruelty and abuse, but it is distinctly the exception and not the rule. At best, it is a trying situation for those in charge; the help upon which they must depend is not the most intelligent, and regrettable incidents occasionally occur.

Yet this whole problem of mental sickness is now receiving so much more enlightened and scientific care that there is no comparison between today's practices and those of even a quarter of a century ago. Those into whose life this sorrow has entered should not dwell too much on the catastrophe. A sickness of this kind is naturally expensive, due to the long time required for cure and convalescence. Nurses have to be provided, constant care must be exercised over the afflicted one, and the illness lasts often for years. Only the quite well-to-do are able to endure the heavy financial strain.

All this the State takes off your shoulders. The best of medical skill is at your service. There are many men serving these institutions who could earn far more in private practice. It is their everlasting credit that they are willing to make this costly sacrifice for the public good. I hold no brief for State Hospitals. If I had my way, I would raze most of them, and I would pay the doctors and the rest of the staff a great deal more than they now receive. I don't think the service is perfect and even the few cases of brutality that occasionally come to light could be largely avoided. However, this is a wicked world, and the vast majority of patients in mental hospitals have done a lot themselves to bring about the fate that has overtaken them. Sympathy is all right. I don't object to your having a good cry over the situation every now and then. It may do you good, but don't forget that you owe a duty to the living.

I told one mother, the other day, that she should bear in mind that she has still a daughter to look after. To constantly brood about the son, was doing him no good and his sister a great deal of harm. My talk helped this woman a lot, as she afterward wrote me. She was better able to bear her cross after talking with me than before. Her renewed interest in her daughter helped her bear the loss of her son.

So I feel that when I ask you to be reasonable in this respect, I am doing something that will help you very much to get over the present hard bit of road. You have done and are doing all you can for your loved one. You have not cast him out on a cruel world to be devoured by wild beasts. You have done everything a loyal parent or friend could do. You can do no more. Take up your other duties with no regrets of this kind to make life hideous. Insist that your mind purge itself of morbid thoughts and recriminations. Think cheerful thoughts. It can be done and it is no crime to do it. The past is gone. The future alone is yours. Make the most of it.

A new addition to the hospital service with which the public is not very familiar, is the social worker. On the staff of many of the larger hospitals a number of women are attached whose duties are to look after the patient's family; and when he has been returned home to keep in touch with him till his adjustment with the world is complete. At the Hudson River State Hospital, such well-known women as Miss Ruth Morgan, Miss Elizabeth K. Lamont, and others are found on the list of those active in rendering aid to reclaimed patients. It is a comparatively new development of medical service, but it shows that the State is reaching out to avail itself of every opportunity to better its service.

So I would add a word of assurance to those who suffer as much on the outside as those on the inside. Disagreeable stories will come to your ears from time to time. Do not let them disturb you. When patients must be restrained, it is done as kindly as circumstances will permit. The doctors visit any infractions of the rules by interns with punishment swift and condign.

Besides that, the State itself has surrounded the patient with many laws designed to prevent just such unfortunate occurrences. A patient cannot be punished except by the doctor's orders, and the doctor must be present when the corrective measures are applied. The much exploited strait-jacket, for instance, is no longer used in our institutions. A much milder form of restraint, a canvas camisole, takes its place. The law prescribes one hour as the limit for continuous confinement. Another hour may be necessary, possibly more, according to the disturbance of the patient; but each hour ends a period and a report is made to the doctor. On his regular rounds, the doctor himself will see the patient and if he has become sufficiently composed, will order his removal to a general ward.

One must always bear in mind that two or three thousand patients are usually affected by one case of disturbance and they are all on edge as it is. One man, therefore, cannot be allowed to create confusion amongst several thousand, so he must be removed from sight and hearing till his outburst subsides. These sudden upsets occur in the best hospitals and are dealt with very much as you deal with Tommy who happens to be obstreperous this particular evening. He is marched off to bed and the rest of the children are left to play in peace.

Stringing patients up by the thumb, tying them to posts, strapping their arms and putting gags in their mouths belong only to the mystery novel. The strait-jacket, as I have already said, has gone to join the screw press and the rack of the Inquisition. All these delightful instruments required time to bring into action and meant extra work for the attendant, and the latter is not looking for anything that even suggests extra work. So he, too, benefits by the abolishment of such things.

Taking everything into consideration, I think conditions are no worse than should be expected. The salary paid by the State for attendants, keepers, nurses, etc., is none too liberal. The opportunities for agreeable social life after working hours is not the best in hospitals. They are conspicuously isolated in a social as well as a physical sense, and are seldom situated as to be within easy access of the attractions of city life. This naturally narrows the circle from which labor may be drawn. With a few noble exceptions most of the workers in hospitals in the lower ranks are of a migratory class. They drift from one city to another, seldom remaining long in one place. You can hardly blame them for that. It is not a career possessing unrivaled possibilities. There are many other occupations I would prefer myself. So we must not look for a new race of Dorothea Dixes among the employees. Yet compared with the average manufacturing industry, like coal mining, steel making, etc., I should place the average intelligence as high, if not a trifle higher. It is, however, a nerve-wracking occupation; and if occasionally you hear of an instance of brutality, do not put it down as an indication of the average conduct of the hospital, but rather as an isolated case, as in fact it really is.

This much can truthfully be said in favor of both doctors and attendants; all hospitals are shamefully over-crowded. Construction has not kept pace with the growth of population and the increase of mental cases. Thousands of such cases were formerly concealed in the privacy of the home, hundreds more roamed the streets to their own detriment and of danger to the community. Not long ago, one of the demented creatures made several persons drink poison at the point of a pistol and spread a reign of terror before he was apprehended.

Health officers now periodically collect such cases and immure them where they can be properly cared for. This adds materially to the census of State Hospitals, and in addition to that, cases of mental illness and nervous breakdowns have abnormally increased. The machine age for mass production may be all very well, but it is certainly playing havoc with a lot of humans, temporarily at least.

The State has not been backward in supplying funds for new buildings, but it took a long time to convince you Solons of the necessity of such huge sums as eventually became necessary. Nothing can now be done to make up for time that is irrevocably lost, and in the meanwhile, we must put up with the overcrowding as best we can.

It is impossible for the present, at least, to do away with the outmoded buildings on Ward's Island, in Binghamton, Utica, Tonawanda and other places. I presume the vintage of these buildings goes back to Civil War days or before. Still, the fact that Sing Sing was finally rebuilt in part makes me hope that perhaps similar action may yet be taken regarding the buildings just mentioned. Following the humane and brilliant example of former Governor Alfred E. Smith, both President Roosevelt and Governor Lehman have interested themselves actively in this direction and the completion of Grasslands, The Pilgrims, Rockland County, and some others rapidly approaching that stage, is most encouraging.

Today there are between sixty and seventy thousand persons in our State Hospitals for mental diseases. That is a staggering figure, but when you come to figure on the total for the whole country you get a figure that is unbelievable—almost five hundred fifty thousand.

The enormous economic loss represented by these figures is hard to compute. The saddest part is that the loss is continuous. Few nervous patients recover within a year, and three years is considered not a long time. Proper feeding and proper housing have much to do with early recoveries, and it is cheaper to give good food and plenty of room than to stint in either direction. At the present writing, the State sins in both respects. The allowance per diem for eating was established before the War when supplies were much less expensive. The reduction in the market prices of all food has improved this situation to a certain extent, but much more is needed before the standard is raised in keeping with the wealth of the States. To get the patient home as soon as possible is true economy. Undernourishment only tends to prolong his detention and quite naturally adds to the expense.

Criticism can be justly made of the overcrowding. That is unquestionably a result of both stupidity and parsimony. This condition was accurately forecast years ago, but, of course, it was treated more or less in the usual fashion of political expediency. Whatever may have been saved by this policy of procrastination has long ago been lost if there ever was economy in the delay to begin with. Governor Lehman, however, has made a thorough personal examination of this state of affairs in New York and I know is doing all in his power to hasten construction, but you can't build and equip a hospital in a day.

It might be a good idea to think a little about the origin of many feeble-minded patients. I am of the opinion that our own crass stupidity regarding the most elemental principles of procreation is largely to blame. We pay Miss Dangerfield, of Kentucky, a huge fortune every year in order that race horses may have the proper dams and sires. The National Government spends huge sums every year telling the farmer how to raise hogs, breed cows, etc. The human race is left to propagate according to its own sweet will. If you ever saw the miserable specimens that I did, mentally and physically, and realized that this human trash had already brought two or three of its own kind into the world and would add more later on, you would begin to understand.

Another lovely fact is that in any one of our Criminal insane Hospitals a patient goes free of the law the moment it is certified to the Court that he is not well. He must be promptly discharged from the institution, as it is always overcrowded and room is needed. No matter what his crime—murder, robbery, arson—he goes absolutely free of the law. The proven murderer must go out and do murder again before the State will take him into custody. Meanwhile he is creating more of his breed at a terrible rate, as every block provides him with a wife.

Out of thirty young women recently sentenced to Bedford Reformatory, great surprise was manifested when only twenty-eight presented the State with new citizens during the brief time of their incarceration. The other two were paroled. In our State Hospitals the number of women at the peak of their child-bearing capacity—between twenty and thirty—totals many thousands. At least one third of them will be returned to society each year. One of our doctors with whom I discussed this subject, cited child marriage as an excellent breeding ground for mental cases.

"In 1930 the number of marriages in which the bride was sixteen, was 230; fifteen years, 197; fourteen years, 33; doubtless, many of them were less than fourteen, but that is the minimum age for girls in New York State.

"We need not shake our heads and say, 'Oh! Foreigners.' Of the sixteen-year-old brides, only ten were foreign born; of the 220 remaining, 153 were of American parentage, 55 of foreign, and 12 of mixed.

"I certainly think that the State could handle the marriage question better than that. Child marriages are not good for the body politic. No board of eugenics would permit such a thing. If we are ever going to stop a large part of preventable madness, we must begin at the source, and here is one source that could easily be dried up."

The talk wandered to eugenics. "Some day," he said, "the Government will pay as much attention to raising babies as they do to raising cattle today, but you and I won't live to see it."

>>>>>>>>>>>>>>> Chapter Five <<<<<<<<<<<<<<

Modern Technique of Mental Healing

I had now been ill for eighteen months and the doctors began to feel very dubious about my ultimate recovery. The question of whether I should be sent to the scrap-heap or kept going a little longer was up for discussion. When it appears to the entire staff that your illness is chronic, the verdict consigns you to the institution where hopeless wrecks are sent, there to remain until that time comes when some orderly tips off a boot-legging undertaker that there's "a new stiff up at the works," and pockets five dollars as his reward.

News of the staff meeting reached me by way of the Associated Grapevine Press, that mysterious channel of communication which exists in all prisons and asylums. It did not interest me particularly. I think one gets callous in a hospital in spite of one's self. When I first saw a couple of young fellows "transferred," knowing what it meant to these boys, I was quite sympathetic. I was actually sorry, but after a while, I thought nothing about it. "It's just too bad," I caught myself saying, and later on, I didn't even say that. I just checked them off my list of specimens and promptly installed their successors. The dreadful fate to which these men went bothered me not at all.

"You had a close call," said the head of the staff, referring to this meeting, as I lunched with him the other day, "and I wish I could remember now just what saved you. It was something you said, but just what that something was I cannot now recall."

That interested me greatly, and I pressed him for details. There's a fascination about discussing some other fellow, who is you all the time, and you can say and think a lot of things that you wouldn't under ordinary circumstances.

"The vote to send you to the incurable ward was heavily against you, nineteen to two. Your history was certainly discouraging. The best we could do for you brought no response. According to the record, you were worse, if anything, than when you came in. Your age was also against you, but every little while some chance remark you made was vastly interesting. We looked for something behind the remark, not the language wholly, but what it indicated. The indications to me seemed to show that behind the curtain that seemed to cloud your brain, there were evidences of a growing desire to break through the curtain. If these manifestations continued and became more frequent, it would show that the struggle to penetrate the gloom would in time succeed."

These may not be the exact words that the doctor used, but that to me was their meaning, and on such a slender thread hung my fate.

If there is one chance in ten, or in a hundred, modern psychiatry will take the chance, and as all the staff agreed there was certainly some ground for the head doctor's opinion, the younger men deferred to his more experienced judgment, and it was finally decided to keep me awhile longer and see if the favorable symptoms would increase or disappear.

I shudder to think what would have happened but for the occasional periods which ensued and which clearly revealed a lost soul struggling, however feebly, for a way out.

The period I am now describing was not a short one. I should say that it extended over a period of at least six or nine months. There were days when it seemed as if all the gain had been lost and other days when it appeared as if progress had far more than overtaken the lost ground. There is apparently no such thing as a sudden clearing up. The illness was a long time coming and naturally was a long time going. It seems to follow the course of an average illness. A person comes down with pneumonia. He doesn't get up the moment the crisis is over; he is very weak, his strength must be brought back and his whole system built up again ere he can return to his normal life. In cases like this, we are trained to expect that the period of convalescence will be more or less prolonged and take it as a natural situation. In mental illnesses we know so little about them that we can't tell exactly when the disturbance has run its course and when convalescence begins. The doctors know, but the patient doesn't. They also know the road to recovery is strewn with pitfalls and for some reason or no reason, relapses frequently occur. The return journey is not without ups and downs.

I do not now recall that I was ever muddled in my thoughts, but I certainly suffered from a depressed state of mind that was so severe as to make me utterly indifferent to muddles or no muddles. In that state you seldom speak to anyone, and then only to snarl. A constant state of hostility would perhaps define the attitude.

About this time I became conscious of a curious discovery—that every one of us possesses a tremendous amount of unsuspected reserve strength. Though I suffered keenly, there were others who suffered still more. Physical pain is bad enough, but mental pain is a thousand times worse, and how some of the poor fellows were enabled to carry their burden would have been utterly impossible but for the possession of this reserve strength. I imagine that it is this reserve strength, working all the time to replace the natural strength that has broken under the strain, that eventually brings the cure. There are no medicines administered, no sleeping potions, drugs or liquors used—nothing but well regulated hours, good food, exercise and a moderate amount of occupation. That is all there is to "treatment." No operations or surgical work of any kind can give relief to a mental patient. He stands or falls largely as the result of his own exertions.

So, in going over this convalescent stage, I am unable to say that any one particular thing brought about the cure. As the spirits lightened, the physical body improved in weight. My weight went down from 180 to 113 pounds. After staying at the latter figure for the better part of the first year, it began to increase, a half pound a week at first, gradually increasing to about a pound. Some weeks I'd slip back and lose all I had gained for a month. Then I would make a surprising gain for several weeks and recover all I had lost. We were weighed every morning and great importance was attached to gain or loss. Some patients fearing loss—which entailed no penalty, but a possible change in diet—would fill their pockets with billiard balls or any other weighty substance that could be concealed. These subterfuges rarely escaped the eagle eye of the charge nurse, who simply relieved the patient of his excess baggage and took no further notice of the incident.

I can now understand the significance of gain or loss in weight in certain cases. There are, of course, many cases where weight remains stationary. One of the tragedies of mental trouble is the fact that physically the patient is often in the pink of condition. Where there are no organic complications this mental illness has not the slightest effect on the physical body. Superabundant health is frequently the possession of the most discouraging cases, but is of great help when the trouble begins to show signs of disappearing. Furthermore, all this talk of superhuman strength in a patient is the sheerest nonsense. There wasn't one of the attendants, and none of them were of the more than usual huskiness found among young men below thirty, afraid to tackle any patient who might become temporarily disturbed or had any fear of them whatever.

Curiously enough, patients seem to retain a respect for authority in most cases.

These varying changes in weight, therefore, always produced a feeling of elation when a gain was recorded and a corresponding blueness when the reverse was the case. I did not then see, as I do now, that the mere fact that I was interested in these changes was a significant sign of impending recovery. It never even dawned upon me, until constant gains had been going on for several months, that weight had anything to do with the case. The first thing that got me thinking along the right channel was when I suddenly had a bad week and lost a couple of pounds. I remember that it gave me quite a jolt. When the next week showed a good gain and the next, it finally got through my thick head that I was getting well, or why this gain in weight? Sickness had sent me down; I was now on the up and up. I watched these figures with constantly increasing interest and when I compared one week with a week, say three months previous, and found almost a gain of ten pounds, I began to sit up and take notice. Yet what was of more importance and which I overlooked entirely, was that I was at last interested in something and that the fear of going out into the world again had to a certain extent lost its terror. Once the idea took hold of met that I was going to be well again, I kept thinking along that line and forgot all the black inhibitions that had formerly held me in subjection.

I do not now recall any time when I did not think clearly. I am conscious of the fact that I did not care to talk to any one and that it annoyed me to have any one attempt to enter into conversation with me. I was perfectly aware at all times of everything that was going on around me and do not recall a single moment when I was confused or didn't know what I was doing. I do know that I was simply sick of living, that nothing interested me. Hoover was elected weeks before I knew anything about it, though newspapers were delivered in our hall every day. The things that formerly interested me failed to possess any further attraction. The only exception to this rule was the stock market. I saw prices rocketing sky-high and it seemed the height of absurdity to me. There was no rhyme nor reason in it to my mind and I actually went as far as to send notes to some friends whom I thought were dabbling in stocks that they were cuckoo to buy at such prices; that up here where we had *sense*, the whole thing was vastly amusing. I further proffered the advice that if they had any of that fancy lithographed stuff that cost a cent a sheet to print and was now selling at a thousand dollars per sheet, to sell out at once. Being a so-called nut, that advice was disregarded and most of these sane (?) friends dropped hundreds of thousands.

Away from the turmoil of the outside world, it was quite natural for a man in my position to realize that the stock market showed that all the crazy people were not in Bloomingdale by a long shot. From where I sat, it seemed perfectly clear to me that I was witnessing a mental disturbance in the stock market that was little different from the hallucinations of those about me. One man, who lost $65,000, still has the letter I sent in a vain effort to save him, so I could produce corroborative evidence if necessary. So much for one lucid interval that I can clearly recall.

Nevertheless, my frightful mental depression persisted. It was utterly impossible for me to dispel the gloom. I could discuss certain business matters, but I seemed unable to take action or do anything about them. The power to work, the will to work, was temporarily gone, and when you no longer care to work or can't work, life has lost its savor. There is no blessing, vouchsafed man, so precious as work and none so lightly esteemed. When once that power is gone woe indeed to the victim.

I am trying, in these notes, to describe with meticulous exactness just what happened to me during this temporary aberration. Apparently the mind is something apart from the brain. A sickness of the mind is wholly a thing apart from a sickness of the brain.

The brain is something tangible on which the doctors and surgeons can operate. In the case of syphilis, for instance, the doctors now inoculate the patient with the germs of malaria. These germs attack and destroy the syphilis germs and the portion of the brain which has been attacked by the syphilis germ is cleared of the enemy and is healthy again. In the case of a sick mind there seems nothing to do but wait and let nature take its course. However, there appears to be a remedial force in nature which starts its work at once and never lets up. It can be tremendously aided by the patient himself if he looks at it in the right way; but while he is suffering he usually is not only willing to help, but does all he can to feed the depression by his own thoughts.

Looking backward at my own experience, I am not inclined to blame the patient much. He is so absolutely miserable that there is nothing to do for the moment but mope. That is directly antagonistic to the policy of the doctors. They want him to be doing something, they want him to weave baskets or set type in the print shop, or read. Anything but mope. However, when a man can't do any of these things, the effort to do so, in my opinion, is an unnecessary strain on a mind already reduced to a point of exhaustion. There will come a time, I know, when that reserve force I have mentioned will make itself felt. It will be very faint at first, hardly perceptible, like the first flutter of the heart in a case of rescue from drowning; but the heart beats gradually grow stronger till they finally become normal. So I think it is in the working of this reserve force. It is hardly noticeable at first, but once it begins it never stops—provided always that the patient cooperates, but it takes a long time to note any improvement. The patient can't see it at first, but it is there. The doctors know it and speak encouragingly.

This period of recuperation seems to me to vary according to the age of the patient. Young people, just out of college, who have collapsed from over-study or over physical training—track work, rowing, football, etc.—are not long coming out of it. Older persons and especially those well in their sixties, have a much more protracted period ahead of them owing to the depreciated condition of their reserve force. Yet there is no doubt that they will all come out of it eventually. If you can get that thought in the patient's mind, you have gone a long way to insure recovery.

It is no easy matter to rid their minds of that awful fear that they "will never get well." Some of them cling to that as if it were a priceless possession. I took a certain satisfaction in it myself, yet I don't know why. I just didn't want to get well. I would much rather be dead. I imagine I fought returning health with as much energy as I could command, but even that cycle ended and nature finally conquered.

I have no doubt that many of my readers have loved ones similarly afflicted and are terribly discouraged to encounter in them the frame of mind I have just described. To them I would say, be not dismayed. That is only one of the phases of the illness and is not permanent. The road may be long and very weary at times, but it's a long lane that has no turning and as sure as the sun sets in the west, the turn in that road will be found and everything will be as it should be. I *know*. I've been through it. You are not reading the words of a theorist or even a doctor. You are listening to a man who tells you what happened to him and he was doubtless a much worse case than the one you have in mind. So don't be downhearted. Cultivate patience and then more patience; inoculate your friend with courage and drive out fear.

You are, no doubt, extremely interested to know exactly the gradual stages by which I approached normality. I am going over in my mind the subtle changes that began to manifest themselves. There was no sudden transformation, no instant recover. Looking backward it now seems to me like the subsidence of a great storm at sea. The howling wind has died down, the tumult of the waves seems spent and the tossing billows gradually sink to rest; only the gentle ground-swell remains.

A glorious feeling of tranquility—a long absent sensation—makes a brief visit. Alas! It disappears only too soon! The old troubled state returns. Yet that sudden surcease was fraught with great importance. If I experienced it once, I argued, it might again return. And with that slight ray of hope came another encouraging symptom. I was no longer hopelessly bound by fear—the fear that I would never be well again. I knew I *had* been well, if only for a few brief moments, and I saw no reason why I should conclude that the clouds would not lift again and perhaps for a longer period.

The one thing needful for a man in this situation is to be brave. His first duty is to subdue fear. His very thoughts are false till he gets fear under his feet. I remembered reading somewhere something on this subject. "A man must and shall be valiant," it said, "he must march forward and acquit himself like a man. Now and always the completeness of his victory over fear will determine how much of a man he is." I seemed to be well enough to understand the significance of these thoughts and fear suddenly became to me not an intangible superstition, dwelling in a mystic, unreal world; but a concrete, living, everyday substance that could be attacked and routed like any other physical entity. Through my muddled mind I could dimly recall having heard many persons say, "Oh! I fear I am losing my mind." They never did lose their minds any more than I did, but fear got the upper hand.

This struggle to conquer fear was a bitter one. To return to the world meant facing a terrible ordeal. Life just couldn't be faced, that's all there was to it; but there is that within us which forces us to do things and gradually this force makes itself manifest. By gradual stages, so gradual as to be almost imperceptible, the mind becomes tolerant to the idea of living again. If encouraged by the patient himself, this improvement can be materially strengthened. As fear gradually weakens its hold, the mind seems to realize that the fetters that bound it have loosened. I do not know that I argued the matter as succinctly at that time as I am doing now, but I am conscious of a change that became more and more recognizable every day. I was able to sit down for ten or fifteen minutes at a time with comparative comfort. I also began to feel tired after hours of incessant, aimless pacing to and fro. That sensation had been absolutely nonexistent for nearly three years. I must have covered all of twenty miles or more a day as I started around 7 a.m. and kept it up till bedtime, 9 p.m., and never felt fatigue. So it was a pleasant sensation to sit at ease for a little while and to feel the need of, and enjoy a rest after a spell of pacing. Both of these changes accompanied the tranquil intervals which were now becoming more frequent and of longer duration.

It is interesting to consider at this juncture what the effect of a sudden restoration to my old post as Director of the Museum might have been. However, that did not happen, and the answer to this pathological problem, which would have been of inestimable value to science, must ever remain unknown. In cases of emotional upset, if you can put your hand on the specific cause of the disturbance and remove it, the chances are that the trouble will end.

I am now trying to recall, as definitely as I can, just what I think marked the first start toward recovery and what symptoms, if any, appeared. A shock had put me there, and perhaps a shock was needed to get me out. The knowledge that I had narrowly escaped going to the "Hidden Death," as we called the hopelessly chronic ward, *was* a distinct shock. While I didn't particularly care to live, I retain a distinct recollection that I disliked intensely the thought of dying in a madhouse. Those pathetic figures that I had seen disappear, never again to be heard from, now rose before me. I had been granted a reprieve. This thing they call Life was evidently something you couldn't cast off like an old shoe or an old suit. It *had* to be lived!

They say that recovery is wholly the result of your own efforts. I would like to claim credit for a great spiritual triumph, for moral courage unsurpassed, for an achievement almost supernatural, but I can't. I had the choice of two evils. To start life all over again at my age was not an alluring prospect. On the other hand, to make up your mind to live is one thing. To do it when you simply haven't the courage, or the desire, is distinctly another. "What's the use?" kept constantly recurring. How that sentence became literally transposed to have a wholly different meaning and thereby saved me is really my story.

I have often been asked if I experienced any sudden change mentally or physically. I did not. As I have just related, it does not happen that way. It is very much like recovery from typhoid or pneumonia. You do not find yourself cured of these diseases in the twinkling of an eye. Your strength returns slowly and your pains diminish gradually. A long period of convalescence ensues, and it may be many weeks before you really feel like your old self again. Sometimes, when it seems as if the disease has left you, there will come a relapse and all the gain will be lost. Finally, the recovery is complete and you are definitely and permanently well. In mental illness it is very much the same way. The doctors said I took one step forward and two back, at the start. Then the forward movement caught up and passed the backward. It was a slow up-hill process, but always the thought of the dreadful alternative kept me in line.

Fear is one of our strongest emotions. It has two reflexes. In one, you become paralyzed and cannot move. In the other, you do something in sheer desperation. In cases of physical danger, the capacity to act doubtless saves your life. A man in jail in India suddenly found a large cobra, the deadliest of all serpents, sharing his cell. For two interminable minutes it swayed its poisonous head from side to side. The man neither moved nor cried out, but he suddenly seized the cobra and sunk a dagger in its throat.

It was some time before I ceased the "What's the use?" complex. Presently the same idea appealed to me in a different way.

Thinking along that line got me nowhere, so what was the use of keeping it up? When you get to the point where you can argue with yourself, then you are making definite progress; but, of course, at the time you do not realize it. Looking back, I do not see that there was anything more difficult about learning to live anew, than there is in learning a foreign language. For a long time it doesn't seem as if you are making any headway. The verbs, the adjectives, the pronouns seem to you hopelessly mixed up. Yet, at the end of a year you are surprised to find that the verbs, etc., are now quite understandable and you are encouraged by the knowledge that what appeared to be impossible is now quite clear and simple. So to it was with me. Life, that I thought could not possibly be lived again, gradually lost its terror. I even began to think that perhaps there was still a place in the busy world for me. When that thought first occurred, I put it away as the fantasy of a disordered brain. Nevertheless, it was a soothing reflection. When I was a boy I built a whole lot of castles in Spain. It never did any harm to any one, and although I was conscious of something like a guilty feeling, I concluded to again indulge myself quite liberally in this direction. Also, I noticed that when I was busy at this work I was more tranquil and able to remain seated quite a reasonable length of time. I could also talk to the doctor without running around him in circles all the while.

My treatment also underwent a change at this period. I was placed in a ward where the day's schedule was much more strenuous. In this new hall there was something doing every minute. It began right after breakfast. At 8:30 we went out for a half hour's walk, and at nine o'clock were taken to what is called "Occupational Therapy." It is quite impossible for the average layman to understand just what the term Occupational Therapy means, as used in mental hospitals. While its remedial potency is recognized to a certain extent, I am inclined to think that this branch has nowhere near reached the position which it will ultimately enjoy. While it is a recognized department in every hospital and most of them have more or less facilities for its practice, its present plan and scope could be greatly enlarged to the tremendous benefit of the patients.

On the men's side in our Hospital, a large part of the two-hour session was devoted to basket weaving. This ancient and honorable vocation has an interesting history, going back almost to the beginning of civilization. It is one of the earliest accomplishments of man. Before the introduction of machinery, it formed an important source of revenue for countless families all over the world.

Its peculiar adaptability for mental illness lies in its comparative simplicity and its freedom from what you might call exhausting labor. The individual strands of reed weigh practically nothing and a finished basket for waste paper, for instance, is lightness itself. The tools required in working are mainly small clippers and awls. It is an ideal craft for the purpose in hand.

While the work is simple, it nevertheless entails a certain amount of concentration. Then the hands find something to do. It is astonishing what a terrific bore it is to have a pair of hands that are forever idle. You may not realize it in normal life, but the hands are constantly occupied with something. So in basket weaving you not only find work for the hands to do, but the brain must necessarily direct the hands, so we have two forces at work that were hitherto lying dormant. As the patient improves in health, his work becomes more intricate and more interesting. He sees growing before him an artistic and beautiful thing formed of many different rows of colored reeds and presently it takes shape. When the task is completed, he has a nice hanging basket that is an ornament to any room. He may wish to color it brown or blue or green. Soaking it overnight, in a vessel containing the required color, will produce the effect he desires. Small work-baskets for the boudoir also surprise the amateur worker with their grace and beauty when finished. Pride of achievement is no less enjoyed in a hospital than it is outside, and that is one of the great virtues of basket weaving. You need not wait forever and a day before you get results.

It also has this peculiar advantage over many other forms of occupation. Each worker seems to be doing work for the same nature. Patients are extremely sensitive, and if they see one man doing something they think is of a higher quality or requiring more skill, they are sure to feel upset or peeved. They must be made to feel that they are as good as the best or they will mope. So the instructor can truthfully praise each worker since they are all doing the same thing, except that one product is more attractive when finished than the other.

As a basket maker, I was not an outstanding success. I would miss a stitch here and there and go blithely on. When the error was pointed out and I was directed to undo all the strands I had woven till I reached the defective part, it was annoying. Usually, the mistake was found almost at the very beginning, never just a strand or two from where I was working, and the result would be a solemn referendum on my part. Would I retrace my errant finger steps, or would I cast the offending basket across the room? I usually did the latter, to the vast annoyance of our dear teacher who frequently proffered the kindly information that he would like to break my neck.

I do not look back on my basket-weaving career as one of unalloyed brilliancy. Occasionally I did do exactly as I was told to do, but that usually created such a commotion that it was deemed wise to transfer me to the Print Shop "for the good of the service."

While I cannot say that I was a shining success in the Print Shop, I did study a lot of words in the dictionary, the exact meaning of which I had long desired to know. In this diversion, I suffered no interference, so my perusal of Noah Webster's great literary performance was greatly enjoyed. Aside from the fact that he changed his subject quite frequently, which did not annoy me, I found many thrills in his monumental work and it apparently suited the disjointed state of my mental muddle at the time. In addition to my dictionarial researches, I also folded circulars, inserted silk cord in dance programs, told the boss printer just how he should run his department and insisted that he use the word "illness" instead of "disease" in the medical reports he was printing. The printer thanked me for my solicitude, but remarked audibly to no one in particular, that it would be a good idea if some persons would mind their own business.

The smell of benzine and printer's ink had a tonic effect upon me. I have been mixed up with type and presses all my life, and I think the old familiar smells were to me highly therapeutic. It seemed to me that I was improving. I also began to linger over some of the pages in the books I was repairing, and that, too, was a good sign. I even peeked into the end of the story occasionally to see if his love had grown cold or if the villain still pursued her.

These were all signs of a slow but progressing recovery. Trees are in no hurry to put on leaves after a long Winter, and the green grass does not come up overnight.

As Spring advanced, the call of the great outdoors made itself felt and I made application to be transferred to the Outdoor Squad and joined the solemn agriculturists who raked leaves, planted vegetables, which never came up, and leaned on their hoe handles meditatively by the hour. Occasionally, as if in a spirit of kindly encouragement or unconscious sarcasm, some of the tomato vines would actually bear fruit! What each tomato cost the State, I do not know. Probably in this respect they ranked with the product of the average gentleman farmer. The late Senator William M. Evarts told his guests to help themselves freely to his milk or champagne, whichever they preferred. "They both cost the same," he would add ruefully.

I sometimes toyed with a heavy stone roller on the tennis courts, that was supposed to level the dirt. When I got through, I had all the neatly trimmed edges of the lawn showing deep indentations where the roller refused to stop and I always managed to bend the net poles at the side of the court in sundry places. When I got through, it looked as if an airplane had made a forced landing. However, since it was the court used by the doctors, I viewed the devastation with huge satisfaction.

Later, however, I got more than a Roland for my Oliver. I was at that time under "C.O." (constant observation) and the attendant detailed to watch me was a green hand just landed. His instructions were to see that I shoveled snow off the sidewalk. Now the regular attendants knew that we would shovel off a spoonful or two, contemplate the surrounding scenery for half an hour and forgetfully put the shovel against a tree. Then we would form part of an audience intently observing some other gang at work. But this new hand didn't understand that mode of conduct at all. He had been told to see that I shoveled snow and that's what he proposed I should do. In vain I expostulated, trying to explain that I was not supposed to do any *real* work. He was obdurate and insisted that I keep on shoveling. As he was much bigger than I, there was nothing else to do; so I shoveled like a good fellow until the path was clear and I was all in.

Baseball as well as golf is designated as "treatment." Some hospitals substitute ditch digging and sewer building for sports as treatment. Once in the Outdoor Squad, I helped wheel bricks from one building to another and I remembered that old gag of Harry Kernell, which may be recalled by some old New Yorkers reading these pages.

"I was up at Bloomingdale the other day," said he, "and I met a man pushing a wheelbarrow upside down" (Bloomingdale was then where Columbia University now stands, so audiences were familiar with the institution, "and I said to him, 'My good man, that is not the way to use a wheelbarrow. You should turn the other side up.' "

" 'Not on your life,' said the man, 'if I did, they would fill it with bricks.' "

However, to return to baseball. One afternoon I witnessed the funniest game I ever saw in my life. The bases were full and the batsman whacked a grounder to short-stop. All four men started to run. Shortstop threw to first, but the ball went wild. Retrieving it, he threw to third, but missed it by a mile. All four men were now running when the umpire cried "Foul," which caused the four men to run back again. This error was corrected, but the runners started again, this time being joined by the batter up, who got tired of waiting for the pitcher to start. To make confusion worse, the runners, instead of stopping at the home plate, continued to circle the bases. The infection spread. All the others waiting to bat joined the runners, who immediately were reinforced by the outfielders, and then by the infielders; some ran one way, some another. In vain, the physical instructor tried to get order out of chaos. The spectator-patients added fuel to the flames by wildly cheering. Pretty soon everybody on the grounds was running around something, somewhere. It was very funny and the laugh I got out of it did me good. I forget just how it ended. They may be running yet.

Golf was also a part of our "treatment." I will spare the reader a recital of a jolly foursome under such gruesome conditions. I was constantly in trouble with the golf instructor, who finally ruled me off the course due to my invariable habit of walking after my ball as soon as I shot it. This was supposed to expose me to great danger from the balls of the other players who followed me. On appeal, I showed the Medical Staff that directly in front of the tee was the only possible safe place on the grounds. The diagram I drew to illustrate the correctness of my contention was rather interesting, if I do say it myself. I was reinstated, on the promise to stand five feet in the rear of the other players, and was immediately hit by a ball that was struck by the heel of a club and spun backwards.

Quite a few patients played the game by themselves. They would have no partners nor join in a foursome. There was less quarreling than happens outside, as a rule. A golf club is a formidable weapon, yet I never saw one used offensively all the time I was a member of the club.

After the morning classes in agriculture, basket weaving, English classics, etc., all students leave the Occupational Department for the gymnasium, promptly at eleven. Occasionally we were delayed. Some particularly timid shrinking violet would secrete some deadly tool on his person, meaning to use it a little later on his jugular vein, and we would be detained till the missing item was recovered. An inventory of all tools, at the conclusion of a session, is part of the morning's curriculum. With this little *faux pas* adjusted, we now proceeded outdoors, being carefully counted as we emerged. This ceremony was an essential part of every gathering. Once a patient, on the way to the hydrobath, hid in a discarded wardrobe temporarily stored in the corridor through which we passed. His absence caused a frightful turmoil. No one had seen him disappear. He couldn't have leaped the fence or escaped through the woods; he would have been seen at once. Finally, after the entire place had been turned upside down, he calmly walked out of his hiding place highly pleased with the commotion he had caused. This was his idea of humor. To this day, I involuntarily count all the passengers who enter an elevator with me or who leave my car.

During favorable weather the setting-up exercises in the gym class were held in the open. In cold weather we went indoors. "Exhale!" "Inhale!" used to drive me frantic. If our physical instructor hadn't been a real decent sort of an Irishman, it would have afforded me exquisite pleasure to cut him up into small bits.

Inside the gym, we played volleyball, basketball, billiards, pool, and had two splendid bowling alleys. Then there were medicine balls, chest expanders, rowing apparatus, swinging trapezes, a short running track, shower baths, etc. It was a very complete and up-to-date gymnasium.

To the average layman it will probably seem as if we were a highly pampered group of goofs. He may not also be able to understand why a wealthy patient, grateful for the kind treatment which he received in this Hospital, should show his gratitude by the presentation of such a magnificent building and its costly equipment as the gymnasium I have just described. Such is, nevertheless, the fact, and it is a nice thing to think about. On the women's side was an equally beautiful structure, the gift of a friend. That was a wise use of money.

This considerable expenditure for what may seem a non-utilitarian purpose, is, on the contrary, a most important influence in the treatment of mental cases. In the summer, much time can be and is spent outdoors, but the long Winter days must also have their diversions. Experience has shown that regular physical exercise is most important. A great many patients can be handled at one time in a building of this kind and the dreariness of a long idle day is much relieved. In addition, radios, phonographs, and pianos all play their part nowadays in hospital life, and none of them are without this valuable addition to their other facilities. The beneficial results arising from their installations proves beyond question their great healing value. Hospitals move slowly and where the public purse is concerned, no money is appropriated except for the most urgent necessities; but having once demonstrated their value, it is only a step to their adoption. Music stands high in the new school for indoor diversion, as do games and other sports for outdoor treatment.

This outdoor work, sports included, is an essential part of Occupational Therapy. It has a definite place in the treatment of patients and apparently has high remedial value. All hands, except those physically unable or disturbed, engage in games or occupational work of some kind. Even those who cannot leave the wards have work of some kind brought to them. To keep the hands busy at something and the mind employed in directing it, has a healing tendency and is quite helpful in distracting one from depressing thoughts, for the time being. I became quite interested in these various departments of O.T. as time went on, and I studied them carefully, particularly the indoor workers.

I soon observed that the patients who made the most rapid mental improvement were also the ones who did the neatest and most artistic basket work. This is what the doctors expect as a result of this work and it is what they strive for—coordination of the mind and body. There is no doubt in my mind that both claims rest on solid foundation.

The Art Metal Department and the Carpenter Shop had far more advanced scholars. They used edged tools and blow-torches and were permitted small fuze fires. Any of these possessions in the hands of men entirely sane draws no comment, but in a cuckoo house their presence denotes a condition of convalescence of great significance. The patient is a long time reaching this dizzy eminence and this public expression of confidence in his mental improvement is equivalent in a sense to the Congressional Medal for distinguished service.

There were quite a number of trades or occupations with which you could dabble in the Occupation Department. In addition to the basket weaving, which was the most important, there was printing, binding, typesetting, brushmaking, cabinetmaking, the making of brass novelties, pipe racks, tennis nets, ash receivers, etc. Quite a variety, you will say. This, however, does not include the women's side, which had entirely different equipment in some respects, but on the whole was practically a duplicate of the men's side.

Naturally, I was not allowed on the women's side. I came to know something of the excellent work done in their department after I came out and saw other hospitals, as well as ours. This work is much more important than I have been able to make clear to you, I fear. I am inclined to believe that it marks the very distinct line between custodial care and remedial care—an important difference in mental cases. For me it has come to have a great personal interest, because I can see where many of us outside can be of practical help in getting these poor people out of the dark shadow with very little effort and scarcely any expense.

At present, the State furnishes the material such as silk, mercerized cotton, wool, linen, patterns and other necessary items needed for this work. Finished work is bought by the State and used in the hospitals. Small rugs, curtains, cushion covers, samplers, paper baskets, clothes hampers and numerous other articles are among the items purchased. The proceeds of this sale are credited to this department and the money is used to replenish the raw materials for new goods. In this way the department is able to provide most of its own capital.

I would like to see an arrangement whereby the State would allow the workers to share in the proceeds wholly or in part. In some of the later built hospitals, as at Orangeburg, a general store is now run in connection with the institution. They sell, at practically cost, a large line of little knickknacks that are in a sense luxuries, such as ice cream, candy, toilet articles, etc., besides little dainties that are not provided by the hospital itself. Persons having relations or friends can leave whatever money they wish their people to have. This is deposited with the cashier. When they wish to go shopping, they apply to the office for such cash as they need and it is given to them and a receipt taken. They then go out with an attendant, unless they have parole, in which case they go alone, and get what they want.

Few of these patients have money and their friends and relatives are similarly situated. If they could receive for their own use, all or part of the money derived from the sale of the pretty articles they make, I know positively that it would add an interest to their work and be of the greatest possible remedial value. I am giving this matter careful study. If I find that my scheme is practical, it will in a measure redeem the three years that went out of my life as a result of my sickness and I would like to recover them if I can.

Those of my readers who would like to become interested in this really worthwhile work, or who would like to become in a modest way possible customers for work of this kind, are cordially invited to write to me. I will gladly answer any letters or be of any assistance I can. It does not call for any heavy contributions from any one and for whatever money you spend you receive good value in return.

I am quite sure (and in this conclusion I am happy to state that I have the practical approval of the doctors with whom I have discussed the project) that the patients will benefit very much in a remedial sense. It will create an interest in their work that has never existed before, and once you get patients where they can work, when they realize that they are working with a definite object in view, you have gone a long way toward arousing interest and starting them on the way toward a new life.

Some legislation may be needed to carry out this plan, but if so, I feel sure it will be forthcoming. A speedy restoration to economic life is the cheapest cost to the State, and Governor Lehman, whose interest in this particular branch of hospital work is especially keen, will, I am sure, cooperate to get the needed laws.

While I have dwelt somewhat extensively upon the routine of a hospital in the more genial months when outdoor life can be enjoyed, this does not meant that during the winter months there is a complete cessation of activity. On the contrary, the cold weather has its obligations, treatments and diversions just as much as the warm.

Our Drama League gave us several performances during the season in the Assembly Hall. These amateur theatricals were all right, except that the players always forgot their lines, spoke out of turn, constantly tripped over something and made their entrances and exits just when they were supposed to do the opposite. One of the doctors, who played the violin, always had to have a scene where he could display his talent; so every act ended with "Oh, here come the merry villagers. Now let us dance and sing," and the good old medico swung into action with both barrels and gave us "Old Dan Tucker," Oh, Susanna," etc. It reminded one of a first night at the Follies, it was so different. The play was usually produced under the direction of the physical manager on the women's side, a close student of calisthenics and the Swedish movements, which accounted for the grace and beauty with which the performers collided with the scenery going out and coming in.

In addition to the indoor gymnasium work, the winter treatment included moving pictures, concerts, dancing, bridge and an occasional afternoon devoted to parlor games. Around the holiday season, special tea dances and private theatricals were offered.

I do not recall anything that was so annoying to me as to witness moving pictures under such distressing circumstances. It never occurred to me that a great many patients were sufficiently recovered as to make these pictures a great assistance to them in their convalescence. As usual, I thought only of myself; but the rules were strict, and all who were physically and mentally fit were obligated to be in the audience. So I had to content myself with shutting my eyes half the time and the other half in trying to figure out how I could hit the charge nurse a poke in the eye and get away with it. One of our number distinguished himself by standing up till all the women were seated. This act of gallantry did not commend itself to the management, so he was asked to remain in his room. The movies were popular—as popular as movies can be, when taken as medicine—and care was taken by the censor not to show anything "sexy." A prolonged kiss, unlike the prolonged bath, made a popular appeal, but was apt to be received with altogether too loud and vociferous applause and be the cause of an incipient riot.

In many hospitals it is impossible to permit the association of the sexes even in such a public place as an assembly hall, though it be directly under the supervision of many doctors and attendants.

It is simply not done, and some of the yarns I heard in explanation of this virtuous attitude would not bear retelling. However, in ours such a drastic attitude was unnecessary. Only selected patients attended these social functions.

At the dances the women patients were frequently in toilettes that were strongly reminiscent of other days and other places. The contrast made me wince, and the strains of "Money Musk" and "Turkey in the Straw" from the orchestra, often gave me a heartache that I fear more than offset the therapeutic value of the gay and festive evening. Toward the last, however, I changed quite a good deal in this respect and finally resigned my laurels as the champion wallflower of our hall, and handed them gracefully to my successor.

I look back with much appreciation on my association with those young nurses whose duty it was to dance with patients. Their behavior toward me was always natural and unrestrained and they treated me with the utmost courtesy. By no word or look did they betray any concern whatsoever. Their conversation was engaging and calculated to make one's thoughts, for the moment at least, more cheerful. One of them told me she had read all of my books and liked *Macbeth* the best. "Although," she added reflectively, "I thought *Ivanhoe* was a hot baby, too." Women patients also danced with male nurses, but no patient ever ran a temperature from dancing with a male nurse.

I am sorry to say that the criticisms expressed by some of my colleagues concerning the undeniable pulchritude of their dancing partners, were not what these charming young nurses would care to hear discussed in such chaste and refined surroundings as a State Hospital. In such places as the Racquet and Tennis Club or the Meadowbrook Hunt Club, it would have been perfectly all right.

On one occasion, a holiday dance in the Assembly Hall was a scene of animation and color. I remarked to the Directress of the Nursing Staff, herself exceedingly young and personable,

"Doesn't this remind you of a musical comedy with a special number now on, 'Dance of the Goofs'?" She laughingly protested my comparison, so I added, "Don't worry, there are just as many goofs outside as in."

Later on, while dancing, I asked her why she didn't wear her engagement ring. Breaches of etiquette like that are quite permissible in a goof house. "I haven't one," she answered.

Giving her a rather critical and I fear impertinent scrutiny, I remarked, "That proves the truth of my contention of a moment ago."

Three months later, her wedding bells pealed out and I had to reduce my estimate of outside goofs by one.

The Sunday preaching in chapel was often good and sometimes not so good. The choir singing was excellent, and the anthems and choruses well selected. At Easter and Christmas the music was delightful. These young people sang for us with as much interest and enthusiasm as if they were in a fashionable church on Park Avenue. As a mark of my personal approbation, I stuck a cigar in my mouth one Sunday, intending to relax in my pew for a comfortable smoke; but before I could light up, the attendant quietly whispered that it was not good form and sequestered the torch for his own use later.

I did not like to look at the congregation. When a group like that get together, they begin to think, and all their thoughts show in their faces. I would read all sorts of stories in them. I tried hard to follow the sermons, but usually failed dismally. Yet at times they were very soothing. When the minister read in a deep sonorous voice, the Twenty-third Psalm, it was strangely comforting. "The Lord is my shepherd; I shall not want. He maketh me to lie down in green pastures; He leadeth me beside the still waters. Yea, though I walk through the valley of the shadow of death, I will fear no evil; for Thou art with me; thy rod and thy staff they comfort me."

There was something very quieting about this beautiful verse and in spite of myself it seemed for the moment to still the raging tumult of my soul. I did not join in the congregational singing. That was an involuntary act of kindness on my part, as any one who has heard me sing will testify; but I read a good many hymns, many of which I had not seen since I reluctantly accompanied my mother to church half a century ago. It was astonishing how familiar they seemed. I could repeat verse after verse, once my eye fell upon them. One I remember in particular, "Pass Me Not, O Gentle Saviour," and I remembered how Fanny Crosby, the writer, had seen this beautiful world for only six months, then total darkness. She lived to be nearly a hundred years old. In her youth, she was a teacher in that fine old institution the New York Association for the Blind. A young boy in the office was always ready to do all he could for the blind teacher; write her letters, copy her poems and anything else he thought would make her life easier. The friendship thus formed lasted all through their lives, the boy later went to the White House as President Grover Cleveland. When I thought of the heavy cross Fanny Crosby had to bear, my own seemed light in comparison.

They never took up a collection. I always thought that was nice of them. Still it would have been jolly fun to see a plate heaped full of suspender buttons, cigarette stubs, old nails and other souvenirs of devoutness. I've always had an eye for the picturesque.

This chapel service also came under the head of "treatment." Well, your whole life at this time was one glad, sweet song of "treatment." I am not overfond of that word. It covered a multitude of sins. After the service, the clergyman took his place at the exit and shook hands with as many as passed him. It was just as if you were outside.

>>>>>>>>>>>>>> Chapter Six <<<<<<<<<<<<<<

Our Suicide Club

The papers that Summer were full of stories about pole sitters and tree sitters, but we had something much more exclusive—ground standers. Such was a patient who would pick out a certain place, generally near a tree, and stand there all day long like a graven image—erect, motionless and oblivious to all surroundings. He never moved a fraction. Usually his hands hung loosely at his side, sometimes the arms were folded but always the same, solemn, immovable figure with a caribou-like face. He made way for nobody. The birds could build nests in his hair for aught he cared. One thought he was a scarecrow as he stood erect with arms outstretched for hours at a time, all the while making horrible faces. At one time they excited my ardent admiration because I was running around in circles all the time and wanted to stand still, or sit still, or do anything but run; but I couldn't. Finally I ran myself out, but they kept on standing. I used to wonder how long it would be before they would take root and grow into trees. Then I remembered that fools like me can make a book, but only God can make a tree. I used to wonder why he made these men in the first place and thought it was a knock at "He doeth all things well.

I cannot record much about the women. We never came in

direct contact with them, but sometimes we saw a group at a distance on their afternoon walk. Occasionally, our paths crossed and we got a fleeting close up. It was a signal for mutual hand waving, and as near a flirtation as we could achieve. Many were young, some quite personable. I must have been very sick at the time, for they appeared to me to possess about as much sex appeal as a mail order catalogue.

Screaming airplanes, bearing the night mail for the Far West, used to zoom past my window just as sleepy (?) time and started another line of thought, which I regret to state was neither poetic nor romantic. It concerned itself mainly with a mathematical calculation as to how long a body up ten thousand feet in the air would take to descend. If I wanted to commit suicide (not that I ever thought of such a thing) I think I would go up in a plane and jump out. It was also interesting to follow that plane in thought and to imagine it being over the Adirondacks in a few hours, and then across the Great Lakes and finally in Chicago long before I could drop off to sleep.

Which brings me up to what I think was the most interesting and diverting group in the whole hospital—our Suicide Club. To commit suicide in a public institution is by no means an easy accomplishment. It is practically impossible. Yet it remains the favorite indoor sport. The results of failure are distressing. One young chap succeeded in cutting his throat. He actually gashed his windpipe, but the doctor reached him in time. The net result, after so brilliant an effort, was disgusting in the extreme. The doctors inserted a silver tube in his throat. For weeks he lay strapped to the bed so that he could not tear away the bandages. Food was administered by tubes for a while, then it was pushed in through his ribs. Some vital motor chord was severed, thus making him a bed patient for life. He will never walk again.

One or two members jumped from windows, but no window providing a dangerous height is ever left unguarded. The one or two that can be used for this purpose have only a drop of a moderate distance. About the best you can collect from a low window is a broken ankle, and sometimes a broken leg or arm in addition. Luck is seldom with you to the extent that you can achieve a broken neck or a fatal fracture of the skull. A real suicide artist would not even stoop to window jumping today. He would be considered *de trop* save among the proletariat.

The gas route is impossible in a hospital and so is poison. Medical supplies are jealously guarded and none issued except upon written order. None are ever smuggled in. Visitors are required to submit their packages for inspection. Any contraband material—liquor, "snow," or anything like that, results in serious trouble to the would-be philanthropist and in prompt withdrawal of his visiting privilege. Eternal vigilance has reduced this hazard to the minimum.

Incandescent light bulbs do not furnish enough material to produce an effective wound. Cuts on the wrist amount to nothing. They are always promptly discovered and a tourniquet does the rest. When the glass globe is broken and swallowed, the pain betrays the secret and the modern stomach pump will tun you inside out in a jiffy. There is virtually no place in the building where a doctor cannot reach you within a very few moments, and even in case of hanging I have known men to be brought back when life seemed to have been extinct for all of ten minutes.

This urge to commit suicide is something that constantly plagues the doctors. That is why all eyeglasses are collected at night, neckties, suspenders and bathrobe belts, also. It is one of the major problems in all hospitals, but how to anticipate, or how to get the patient's mind off that fascinating pastime, is the question. Generally speaking, the doctors are not fooled very often. In my own case, when I was charged with suicidal mania I frankly admitted that the project possessed an academic interest for me, but beyond that it did not intrigue me. While I was free to admit that life in a cuckoo house did not appeal strongly to my aesthetic nature, yet I was not prepared to exchange the ills I knew of, for those I knew not of. I also advanced the argument that at present I possessed a yellow streak of such imposing proportions that it provided an ample margin of safety against any untoward happening in that direction.

That was dismissed as subtle sophistry upon the ground that physical fear did not enter into the premises at all. With this statement I could not agree. I found out afterwards that I was wrong.

This suicidal complex is one of the really dangerous features of a mental sickness. Many of us have often said, "Oh! I wish I were dead," but never seriously meant it. The feeling that comes over you when mentally ill is altogether different. There is no comparison. The one is a passing emotion, the other is entirely different. There is an utter absence of the desire to live. There is no fear regarding the future, no matter what it may be—it holds no terrors compared with the present. The natural fear of death, which we all have in normal moments, no longer exists. I never got as far as that, but I imagine that if I had been alone anywhere with a high window handy, I would have been strongly tempted. There is no doubt that this mental depression is something unspeakably horrible. It is difficult to find a parallel. I have tried to recall just how I felt, but the only impression that remains is very indistinct and recalls nothing but what you would experience looking down a bottomless pit. I remember, however, a very distinct desire to peer beyond my present existence and see what was on the other side of the door. That curious conception is still clear in my mind. I wanted oh! so much to know what was beyond. I was consumed with curiosity. At first I had a terrible dread that I would like it; yet, if I didn't, there was no retreat. So I would stand still with my hand on the knob, but without the courage to open the door and take the short step that would mark the change from life to death. Then I would slowly and surely remove my hand from the door. It seemed such a slight change to make, and it would mean so much. Why endure this cruel tumult of the mind when peace was within reach? Peace, blessed peace! That seemed to be the one thought in my mind.

There was no wildness in my imagination, no unreasoning devastating power urging me to do something against my will. I was more than a willing accomplice. What was beyond that door? How I longed to know! Why should I not do with my own life whatever I pleased? It was mine—all mine—and if I chose to end it, that was my own business.

There is no doubt in my mind now, that the first law of Nature, self-preservation, had completely broken down. That great factor in all human lives had temporarily disappeared; some icy feeling had taken its place, immune to ordinary sensations, and rising above and beyond everything else was the seductiveness of rest and peace—perfect peace.

Dead men were always quiet. Nothing disturbed them any more. They always looked to me as if they were at rest at last. No matter what their lives—good, bad or indifferent—it made no difference—death was peace and the end of strife and turmoil—an irresistible prospect. I began to argue that it was not murder to kill yourself. I recall a curious incident that occurred in Austria. I think, soon after the Great War. A certain farmer hanged himself. That is to say, he meant to hang himself; but an officious passer-by stupidly, though chivalrously, rushed to the rescue and cut the suspended man from the benevolent tree in time to preserve the life which the farmer planned to destroy.

The would-be suicide thereupon brought suit against the meddler upon the ground that the latter had, with malice aforethought, compelled him to endure a further dose of life which said attempt destroyed his peace of mind, causing him great mental anguish and was contrary to the statutes made and provided; and furthermore, was a distinct assault against the rights and privileges of the party of the first part in his pursuit of life, liberty, and happiness. The jury brought in one of those Scotch verdicts: "Not proven."

A contemplation of the facts in this provided some additional material for my contemplative and argumentative mind. I knew that families felt disgraced when one of their members committed suicide. But why should they? If you give away or destroy something that is wholly yours, whose business is it but your own? There is no analogy, I went on to myself, between murdering yourself and murdering someone else. I can clearly see that in the latter case you are taking something that does not belong to you; in the former you are merely doing what you like with your own. The sweetly sentimental attitude of the public toward the sacredness of human life did not impress me much either. Not with the memory of twenty million lives snuffed out because a crazier man than I ever was took it into his head to find a place in the sun. That, to my mind, disposed of whatever is meant by "sacredness." Nor could I see where society would not distinctly benefit by the removal of myself and, I could truthfully add, most of those about me. When a human being has definitely ceased to be a useful member of society, I see no reason whatever why he should not depart whenever he so desires.

Thoughts like these kept my mind occupied more or less actively during the suicide period. Exactly when they took another trend, is difficult to state. In my experience, there was no immediate, instantaneous change from darkness to light. There was no sudden "snapping out of it." I grew tremendously enraged at that phrase toward the end. Everybody was constantly urging you to "snap out of it." I hope the next man who says it to me will come prepared to meet his God.

We all would have liked to "snap out of it." That's what we most desired, not only out of the suicide complex, but the whole damnable depression as well, of which suicide was only one of the minor by-products. In time, however, the physical system of growing stronger, one was less and less disposed to talk of death all the time. Spring had come, the trees were budding, and in spite of yourself something of the old zest of living made itself manifest more and more as each day went by.

I often look back at these suicide days and wonder if my conclusions were well founded concerning the right or wrong of it. I find myself divided on that question. So far as I am personally concerned, I cannot see wherein I am of the slightest use to the body politic. I may putter around for a while, at considerably unnecessary expense, and possibly write a few things that no one will read except the proofreader. It is too late for any constructive work, and the man who merely clothes his own back and fills his belly has not, in my opinion, discharged his whole duty to society and really isn't worth his salt. What's left is to see some young deb nudge her friend and whisper, "See that man talking to mother over by the piano?" and hear the other one say, "Yep." "Well, he's the cuckoo who wrote that bug-house article our Literary Society was discussing the other day." Not a very wonderful contribution to the world's work when you come to think of it; distinctly not worth the cost of upkeep in these dour days of depression, in my opinion.

Of course, there are other things to be considered—the family for one. It is not a nice memory to leave and it might upset some of the members. That's always a possibility, and in my opinion an "upset" is worse than suicide. We often discussed it in the Club.

Of the dozen or more men like myself who had passed their productive period, it seemed stupid to keep those here who wanted to go. We all ought to have imitated that Austrian farmer and have sued the Hospital for damages, but in this enlightened country, the same legislative wisdom that gave us the Volstead Act has also decreed that a man who attempts unsuccessfully to take his own life, is guilty of attempted murder, and any suit on our part was not only foredoomed to failure but would attract attention to our own escapade.

This suicidal period is on the whole, I think, rather interesting. If the doctors at the Hospital even suspect you have a suicidal complex, a special attendant is immediately detailed to accompany you on all your wanderings. I once innocently discussed suicide in a casual conversation with the supervisor. I maintained that no man in his senses would ever dream of such a thing; that it was no different from plain everyday murder. I made several other lofty and profound philosophic observations, and flattered myself that I had much the better of the argument. I did, but within an hour, orders came to place me at once under "C.O." which means "Constant Observation." Under this beneficent dispensation an attendant is detailed to dog your footsteps from the moment you wake in the morning till you are herded into your room at night. Not for one instant during the livelong day are you out of his sight. His eagle eye is upon you, as his title indicates—constantly. If he happens to be called on to do some little errand elsewhere in the ward, he takes you along with him. So in time you learn all the details of the pantry room, linen room, retiring room and other private corners of a hospital not included in the ordinary curriculum.

"C.O." used to drive me frantic. It would do that to a sane man. Yet, if you informed the genial idiot in charge of you, ever so politely, that if he hadn't sense enough to leave you alone for a breathing space at least, you would knock his block off, it would result in further restriction—a visit to the back halls perhaps, where the furniture is nailed to the floor and the boys walk around in bare feet so that when they kick the shins of the keepers it won't hurt much. It's not at all pleasant there, some of the guests behave worse than poor losers at contract, and are equally rough in speech.

To get rid of this "C.O." sentence, is quite an undertaking. The more you protest, the more the doctor is convinced that he is right in having you watched. In vain, I pleaded for some mitigation of the nuisance, even going so far as to assure them that I was never happier in my life and never wanted to die less than I did at that particular moment. I even offered to tell them another, if that didn't come up to specifications. To all my entreaties they turned a deaf ear; but all things pass away eventually and after a year or so I was restored to liberty. You can get used to anything in this world and it is really astonishing what this human frame of ours can endure.

This rather intimate and personal relation which must of necessity obtain the "C.O." man and his patient is apt to prove irksome if one may speak candidly. There were times when I much preferred the society of the chap, for instance, who always saw beautiful tropical fish swimming past his head and never failed to call my attention to their gorgeous coloring; or the other young man who was continually crying because the people of New Rochelle were starving. Knowing the people of New Rochelle as I do, I callously said, "Let 'em starve."

Thus the days went by, days of deadly monotony, days of bitter memories and vain regrets; and the future was filled with anxious forebodings. Engulfed in a veritable sea of insanity, there seemed no escape. All around were insane people. What a chance had I against such overwhelming odds? A sane man would have had a terrific struggle to maintain his reason in such a place, much less a nervous wreck like myself.

One member of our Club, Chairman of the House Committee, thank God, unexpectedly got a good break. We were on our usual afternoon walk, which led through an unused dirt road in the woods. This particular afternoon the path attracted the attention of a bus driver whose vehicle had been ordered back to the garage for some reason or other. Apparently this road offered a short cut to his home base. As our group came opposite the bus, this enterprising gentleman threw himself under the front wheels which passed over his head. It furnished the rest of us with a new and rather amusing topic during the remainder of our walk. The charge nurse noted on his daily report that Mr. So and So failed to return from the walk. As this rather pretty, leafy bower was henceforth closed to us, I thought it was not cricket on the part of our friend to choose this particularly pleasant path and mess it all up, when there were so many others that would have answered his purpose just as well.

In the case of another member of our Club, I thought he was much more considerate and certainly his conduct was much less reprehensible. Just before "going west" he even declined to help himself from my tobacco pouch when I discovered his was empty, saying that he would "not need any more smokes." I paid no attention to the remark at the time, being engrossed in the game of contract which we were at the moment enjoying. In the morning he was gone.

Sometime during the previous week, at odd moments, he must have surreptitiously worked the heavy screws loose that held the ponderous metal weather screens in place in his ground-floor room. In this ward, being for more advanced patients, they answer the purpose of the more unsightly iron bars. So the way of escape was open. When the stab of the flashlight in the hands of the night supervisor was upon him, he knew that another visit would not be made for an hour and began his preparations.

He must have walked quietly out of the window from the rear of the house to a clump of trees not far distant. His path across the lawn lay alongside a partly used road separated by a heavy picket fence. Knowing the virtuous character of all hospital attendants, he had no fear of encountering any roistering parties at that unrighteous hour.

Imagine what that last, sad journey must have meant! I never could have done it myself. It must have taken a lot of courage. To look up at the stars for the last time, to hear the twitter of a half-awakened bird, the quiet rustle of the trees and know that you would never see or hear them again. No, I never would have been brave enough to do that.

Selecting a tree he must have had in mind, he threw the belt of his bathrobe over one end of a limb. Out of this he made a hangman's noose. In a few minutes he was dangling in the air, and there he hung by the neck until he was dead. Some workmen, on their way to the farm, found him there in the morning.

"O life, O death! O littleness of men
Who shall not pass this way again!"

It was rather an artistic job, and on the whole reflected credit on the Club. The usual resolution of congratulations, with three rousing cheers, was adopted at the next meeting and appropriate recognition made of the skillful craftsmanship displayed in the take-off.

Another member rather dimmed the glory of our tree hanger by accomplishing the same result under much different conditions. He might have been even more highly esteemed but for the fact that he was much below the average height and of exceedingly light build, so perhaps his achievement was not so spectacular as it first appeared. He managed to hang himself in the ordinary clothes press found in every room. They are flimsy affairs at best, but apparently much stronger than I thought. At all events, he managed to drape himself from the hook, usually reserved for neckties, and in the morning was found lifeless. At a subsequent meeting of the Club, full credit was given him for an unusual feat and his name was placed high on the roll of honor. From the remarks of the members it was apparent that he had taken advantage of the momentary confusion which attends the exit of the night force and entrance of the day crew. How he managed to avoid kicking something in the final throes of his death agony, thereby calling the attention of the nurse or one of the attendants, was always a mystery to me. The legs usually twitch spasmodically as the suffocation increases. This often betrays a man and has deprived many a Club member of the honor of securing the much-coveted wooden cross.

At a meeting of the Club one night, I read a poem. It was an atrocious thing to do. I tried hard to resist the fiendish urge, but it was no use. It was greeted with jeers, curses and demoniac laughter, and I gloat over the maddening yells, the imprecations, the sarcastic applause, that marked its reading.

"There is no death; when I pass hence
The waning moon, once more
A crescent boat, before the dawn
Will anchor at my door,
And in it I will sail away
To some far port beyond the day.

But I will be a visitor
To you, although unseen;
I shall come stepping down the stars
Midnight and morn between,
And while you slumber unaware,
Will leave a kiss upon your hair."

Our Suicide Club existed only under conditions of the most discouraging nature and had a hard time to maintain its boasted slogan of a "bump a month." One year it had such a poor record that it was contemptuously referred to as the "Sissy" Club. For a few brief moments, on one occasion, I enjoyed the honor of being a suicide with none of its attendant inconveniences. The Hospital office was suddenly busy with telephone messages from several New York papers requesting particulars of my death, what caused it and so forth. Members of my family were also importuned for information of the same sort and for a day or so I experienced the blissful sensation of being an object of interest to the outside world. One or two obituaries were canceled just in time, so I did not enjoy reading what a perfectly worthy citizen I really was, and that was a great disappointment. I thought it was quite nice to have the papers interested to this extent, and I have often wondered what these obituaries contained. No doubt, they would have been written in a kindly spirit, as we generally receive a bouquet or two when they are no longer of use to us.

Of all stupid things suicide is the most stupid. In my lifetime I recall three distinct occasions when it proved the worst thing to do. C. T. Barney, President of the Knickerbocker Trust Company, is a case familiar to many. His affairs seemed hopelessly involved and his bank failed. He blew his brains out. In less than a year his estate became not only solvent, but his losses, by an upturn in the market following the Northern Pacific crash, had been more than regained.

Another man carried large real estate holdings all through the depression. Taxes were heavy and he finally lost courage and shot himself. Less than a year afterwards the Federal Government bought his land to extend an airport, paying his heirs over a million and a quarter—a sum far beyond his expectations and one which would have made him rich.

The third was a young Britisher, stranded in Shanghai after the War. He had lost everything. He pulled out his service revolver and stuck the barrel in his mouth. At the last moment something of his old time pride returned and he refused to do the cowardly act. Fortune, as if in recognition of his grit, smiled upon him. In a very few months he had entered business and struck it rich. His bank account exceeded a quarter of a million.

No man living knows what a day will bring forth. While there's life there's hope and suicide is so final that the thought must be put out of your mind, cost what it may.

My good friend Dr. Gregory Zilboorg, who was attached to the medical staff during my last semester in dear old Bloomingdale, and later resigned, has since been appointed research director of the Committee for the Study of Suicide, which was organized to make a world-wide study of self-destruction as "a preventable disease."

Dr. Zilboorg told the thousand men and women recently gathered at the Hotel Roosevelt for the fourteenth annual convention of the American Orthopsychiatric Association that the time had come "to discard conventional and time-worn conceptions" of suicide. He said the newer view looked upon suicide as a problem which was as much a natural biosociological phenomenon as war, murder or revolution.

Suicide cannot be prevented even among the most enlightened unless it is considered as a form of instinctive expression, rather than "a mistake of society, a slip of the mind, or a defect or a perversion of nature," he emphasized. "Suicides differ not only in the method of weapon used for the act of self-destruction, but also in the psychological history of the individual and his attitude, conscious and unconscious, toward life and death. The suicidal drive appears to be a real elemental psychic force, universal in nature.

"But our studies of clinical material have not been detailed nor deep enough to trace with clearness and accuracy the psychological texture of the suicidal reactions. Pending further and more thorough study, we must limit ourselves first, to inferential evidence, and second, to a closer inspection of the suicidal habits of primitive races."

As a young man, Dr. Zilboorg was a soldier of fortune and a close and able lieutenant of Kerensky in the early days of the Russian Revolution. He and Kerensky would today occupy the positions held by Lenin and Stalin had their plans been successful. I would a good deal rather hear him talk of this exciting period of his career than listen to his fantastic raving about suicide.

The last I heard of Kerensky was that he was selling life insurance in London.

The way to prevent suicide is to make things for the individual so comfortable and easy that he would rather stay here than go anywhere else. That can be accomplished by living a life according to the Sermon on the Mount, or by suppressing about ninety percent of the present output of psychiatric literature.

At the same meeting Dr. Margaret E. Fries, who has been studying the question of the relationship of parents and children at the New York Infirmary for Women and Children, said that infants only six weeks of age begin to reveal definite trends and patterns of behavior which may make an infant a "problem child" later in life. She recommended psychiatric treatment of parents before the birth of an infant.

A little treatment of both parents before marriage, in a great many cases, would probably prevent problem children from even making their appearance, which would be still better. I'd hate to own an infant that could show "definite trends and patterns of behavior" at six weeks.

Also at this meeting Dr. Lauretta Bender and Adolph Woltman of the Psychiatric Division of Bellevue Hospital reported that the use of puppet shows was proving valuable in helping children to get rid of their worries. In other words, if you haven't anything worthwhile to say, hand out an old bromide that is so obvious and incontrovertible that no one can gainsay it. Some people will then think you are speaking off the cuff.

I must admit that some of the antics cut up by the patients were at times disconcerting. For instance, one of them for whom I had profound sympathy, seemed unable at times to restrain an impulse to swear. His swearing was in a class by itself. It was directed to no one in particular and was undoubtedly an involuntary performance. Promptly after the rousing blast from the morning whistle sounded, he began. At first, I thought it was his matin hymn to that renowned sleep shatterer, but it was altogether too picturesque and to long continued for so mild an offender, figuratively speaking. Much as I cursed that ear-splitting whistle myself, its toot-toot was a paean of praise compared to the performance of my friend. Perhaps he intended to include enough profanity to also cover the mournful dirges that emerged from the entrails of the clock tower which boomed the passing hours. But even that hardly accounted for the ferocity and elaborateness of his vocabulary.

He was decent enough to go off in the farthest part of the hall and be of as little nuisance as he could. When the attacks recurred with unreasonable frequency, he was always good enough to ask, himself, that he be transferred to the back halls where patients were expected to yell their heads off and sing the same verse of the same song for thirty days without stopping.

The Hypochondriacs were another queer dish. You meet plenty of them outside, but not such robust specimens as we have in hospitals. The one in a room not far from me spent most of his time examining a small swelling on his forehead which he was convinced was a cancer in its incipient stage. It was, of course, examined by most of the doctors on the staff, for he would waylay them anywhere he could find them and ask their opinion. They all told him it was a natural contour of the forehead, but that brought no comfort. You can, of course, send for outside medical help if you don't like the decision of the resident staff, so this chap had a procession of them trooping in all the time and each one collected one hundred dollars per visit plus traveling expenses—only to confirm the diagnosis of the Hospital staff.

Then he made up his mind there was something wrong with his tonsils. To satisfy his longing and also to relieve the worry that was doing him no good, they cut out his tonsils. This didn't help as he began to get excited over an enlargement of a joint in the second finger of his right hand. That was certainly something serious at last. He bathed that finger almost every ten minutes, marching all the way down the corridor to the wash room with his towel over his shoulder. Then he got the germ theory. Germs were everywhere. That necessitated more hand washing and his trips to the wash room were increased tenfold.

He wrote his wife that he wanted to come home. Before the letter had time to leave the Hospital, he would write another saying he wanted to stay where he was. Then another, practically besieging her to come at once and take him away, and so on. By the time he got through, his wife had about a hundred notes, each one contradicting the other. Finally she determined to take him home anyhow and end his uncertainty. Then he stopped every one who would listen to him to ask whether they thought it would be wise for him to go or stay. He would agree to any answer you made, and take up the subject all over again with the next man he met.

The "hypos" in the outside world are not quite so pestiferous, but are still quite a nuisance. They do not annoy me so much as the people who are determined to relate every minute detail concerning their last operation. The more operations they can boast of, the greater they appear to be in their own eyes. I imagine they think of themselves as one of these distinguished generals whose chests are covered all over with medals. Personally I would like to cover them with six feet of dirt. For of all the bores that irritate me, the ones who must meticulously discuss all their symptoms, and are everlastingly speaking of operations, are the worst.

The Claustrophobias were quite a nuisance. Put them in a nine-hundred-acre plot and they would still feel suffocated because they could see trees in the distance. Somehow or other they seem able to afflict you with the same choking sensation which they feel all the time, and I felt very uncomfortable whenever they came near me. The strange part of this was the fact that I might be walking or talking with one of the species, but unless I knew the nature of his delusion, it didn't affect me at all. Our imaginations have much for which to answer.

We had, of course, a few cases of Religious Mania, mostly young preachers who had become overenthusiastic. This disorder is quite common in nervous hospitals and though it rages with considerable violence while it lasts, does not seem to be serious. We had one very likable young chap, I recall, who was quite a desperate case at first. I was deeply concerned over him and not a little delighted to see him "snap out of it' (Oh! that phrase) in record time. Some persons get wildly excited over religion. In the old camp-meeting days of my boyhood, I still vividly recall scenes at Ocean Grove that produced a frenzied condition which would rather alarm me today, knowing as I do what too much hysteria of this nature can produce. Most of these front-page evangelists seem to me to be nothing but incipient pathological cases and few of them ever accomplish any permanent good. In our Hospital, our young friend did not force his ministrations upon anyone. He would gladly pray with you, and pray long and earnestly. It seemed to do him good and the patients no harm.

>>>>>>>>>>>>>>> Chapter Seven <<<<<<<<<<<<<<

Joys and Terrors of Visitors' Day

Visitors' Day was to me something like the oldtime country fair. We were all arrayed in our best bib and tucker, freshly bathed and shaved. Our clothing was carefully inspected for possible rips or tears; shoes neatly shined; collars and neckties clean, spotless. Hospitals believe literally that "cleanliness is next to godliness" and soap is considered a means of grace. I think they are right.

That, to me, was at first quite a thrilling experience. It was something new for me to hear a son curse his mother and revile his father; to see a man deliberately turn his back and offer any insult he could think of to the best friend he had on earth—his wife. To see a brother or sister cruelly wounded was not so hard. You've known that to happen outside, but the other seemed more painful, more unnatural. A peculiarity of mental illness is that it turns you against all those nearest and dearest to you in many instances; and I have seen wives, who never knew what it was to hear a harsh word, be utterly prostrated by the shameless conduct of those whose sufferings they came to alleviate. One woman told me, with tears streaming down her face, that she thought she could bear it no longer. "He was the best husband a woman ever had," she sobbed, "till this awful thing came upon him. I don't understand it, I don't know what to do." Her sister, with whom I sat on the bench while the wife visited the husband in a section which was forbidden to me, told me more of the story. The sister was widowed. The two couples were childless, but were a very happy family circle living together. Life had run on in this pleasant, modest fashion for years. Then this thing happened. The radio and mechanical music had cut into his business—pianos. Unwise investments, made in the hope of stemming the tide of misfortune, had turned out badly, and he crashed.

The saddest part of the tragedy was undoubtedly the curious twist his mind took, resulting in the violent hatred he now showed toward the sweetheart of his youth. This is a common occurrence in nervous breakdowns which makes it very hard for the unfortunates involved. They seem unable or unwilling to realize that it is part of the sickness, and it adds immeasurably to the pain already caused by the forced separation and the knowledge that a loved one on whom you gladly lavished every care, must now be turned over to the tender mercies of an unfeeling, unsympathetic attendant with a heart of stone or no heart at all.

One of the sad things about mental illness is the wide circle of persons upon whom it inflicts keen suffering by reason of family ties. Dozens of families sometimes, connected by consanguinity, are involved, and their sufferings are by no means light. One does not need to be the principal in this tragedy in order to suffer, and in the cases where the mischief has been caused by vicious habits or other preventable causes the result to a large number of perfectly innocent persons is just as bad as if they themselves were the culprits. I often think a two weeks' sojourn in a mental hospital at an early period in life, would be one of the best things that could happen to us. It would at least show us the necessity of self-control and teach us that none of us are wholly independent; that our lives are of necessity bound up in others. After all, when you are in really deep trouble, it is your own flesh and blood who stand by you, and it is of them you should think before you take a step that you know is liable to plunge them all into misery. These were the thoughts engendered in my mind by that Roman holiday known as Visitors' Day, a ghastly performance in the main, but a firmly rooted custom in all State Institutions.

There was a gentleman of my own age who caused my wrath to reach the boiling point regularly on this festive day. His wife, a sweet-faced, white-haired, old lady, made a considerable journey every seven days to see her lord and master. That's a queer title to bestow on the derelicts that answered to the names. When she finally arrived at the Hospital, after a long and tedious journey, was she rewarded with a warm embrace and kindly speech? Hardly. On the bench allotted them, he would park his carcass as far away from her as he could. He would then take out a paper and read it all the time she was there. When the time was up, he never raised his eyes or said good-by. I remarked to him one day that if he conducted himself like that again I would give him a first-class beating.

He was an old doctor and had evidently been somebody in his day. Well-known names would drop from his lips and we often talked of the City as we recalled it as boys. He was a strange contradiction, but there were two things he had apparently made up his mind to do, come Sunday, come Monday. One was to wear his heavy winter overcoat in summer and the other was to make an ass of himself whenever his wife came to see him. I forget just what type of illness he suffered from, but he was eventually sent to another place where they didn't care whether he got well or not, so I guess he was pretty sick.

Another of the same type was an ex-service man who insisted on playing tennis while his wife was present. He could play it any time he was so disposed, but he seemed to enjoy it only when his wife was visiting. She got no time to talk to him whatever. He played just long enough to cover the hours she could stay. When she disappeared, his game was at once drawn to a close. Queer, wasn't it? A whole lot of us seemed to have that queer inhibition that rendered us deadly enemies of those who loved us and cared for us the most.

Occasionally, but very rarely, one of those incidents which the blood and thunder novelists like to write about, would turn up—where the heir to the ducal palace is cruelly locked up in a half-forgotten castle, there to eat his heart in silence while the villain enjoys his ill-gotten fortune in apparent safety. There was one young chap, who lacked a few weeks of his majority and who tried to make us believe that he was the victim of some such romance. The truth was that his allowance of five hundred a week, which began when he was nine years old on the death of his last parent, proved too much for him. No matter what you say, my sympathies went out to this boy to a certain extent. He remembered little about his mother and nothing at all about his father. Although he had brothers, sisters, cousins and aunts, none of them had the power to choke off that deadly weekly income, and he was now close to his majority and would be placed in sole control of the principal. Even by this time there was little in life left for him to know, but, of course, he would try to find out for himself what little that remained and the new fortune was large enough to help him in his worthy ambition. So the brothers and sisters locked him up.

They brought him, I think, from a night club in Harlem. He had a predilection for "high yellows," and kept about a dozen of the best he could find. This was quite an ambitious program and taxed even his splendid physique to the limit; for in addition to his other accomplishments he was acquiring considerable skill as an opium smoker and cocaine addict. When they finally got him safely landed in our Hospital, it was quite natural that he should attempt an exit by the aid of the electric light bulbs. Of course, he hadn't a chance on earth, and they caught him before he had time to dig open his wrists. He succeeded in staining the white sheets a brilliant red, but that was about all. Youth and constant observation, combined with a rather intensive exercise program, soon worked the poison out of his system and in three months he was profoundly thankful to be alive.

Once you are "committed" to our regal palace, it is hard—practically impossible—to get out. It is on this fact that all these romances hang. You are held excommunicado, which means that all your outgoing mail is sent to only one place—the person who had you committed. So, of course, the chance of getting word to a friendly accomplice is practically nil, and nothing a patient can do can change that rule. So our young friend, who was anxious to celebrate his coming of age with a party commensurate with the dignity and importance of the occasion, was sorely put to find ways and means to accomplish this end.

By this time he was in fairly good shape. It's astonishing the rapid recoveries these dissipation cases make when they are still in their teens. So he was more than anxious to regain his liberty, but the mailing arrangements were a serious obstacle. Another "rummy," however, whose term had expired volunteered to get him a good lawyer as soon as he was outside, which he did. This legal gentleman showed up at a thousand dollars per visit; made two or three visits and liberated his client by threatening habeas corpus proceedings. Hospitals do not like publicity and avoid it if at all possible. In a few days, the necessary legal formalities were completed and our friend left to enter "business."

He was an easy mark for everybody. He did buy into some concern, but that's about all it amounted to. The other chap got some good money for worthless stock and our friend acquired some experience. A month later, when he received his inheritance, he was on an airplane bound for Hollywood, where he doubtless was received with open arms.

In a place like ours, there are always mysterious rumors floating around of some patient having been railroaded there for the sake of getting him out of the way. I do not know how much truth there was in these rumors. The Hospital, of course, has nothing to do with such cases. They are simply the custodial institution and on an order from the Court must produce the body, dead or alive, of any person the Court demands. I never heard of any real, genuine incarceration for the sole purpose of getting rid of someone, but occasionally such instances do come to light. No doubt, there were numerous cases where the families did not particularly care to have it known that one of their members was there, but in those cases there was no question about the necessity for such incarceration and they were all genuinely ill. There was, of course, no end of gossip concerning those who had been there twenty or thirty years. There were few left who could contradict any legend that might have grown up concerning any particular patient, so it was quite safe to create any kind of yarn your fancy suggested. I remember one chap who had come there as a mere boy around fifteen, I was told. Every week his mother came to see him. Toward the last, her hair was gray and she walked with feeble steps. Soon after she came no more. The boy meanwhile had passed his young manhood and now his temples were white. He may miss his mother, but it is doubtful. I could not help thinking what a long vigil that had been for the old lady, waiting for Reason to come back, and how that willful jade had eluded her.

In all those years, that boy had dressed with scrupulous care. His hair was parted in the middle, as was the fashion in the gay nineties, and his clothes were immaculate. He was always going somewhere and carried a sheaf of magazines under his arm at which he never even glanced, but one was ever open at an unread page. I think some concussion of the brain resulting from a spill from one of those old high bicycles, caused his trouble. Accidents sometimes do that. Rather hard, I thought, to start out on a "century run" and never come back.

One afternoon, after the visitors were gone, but before the patients were shooed into their coops for the night, one of them suddenly swung himself from a low-hanging branch on to the trunk of the tree and in a moment had climbed to the top. Great excitement immediately ensued. A ring of attendants surrounded the tree in the desperate hope of in some way or other catching the patient when he jumped. It was, of course, taken for granted that the sole purpose in view was suicide, but what possible good the ring of attendants was, I could not see.

A brilliant thought struck someone. Mattresses were collected from all quarters and soon formed a circle of softness around the tree. On account of the branches, he could not very well clear the mattresses, and the chances were that they would break his fall.

Finally, one of the attendants started up the tree. If he did not get his head kicked off, he might possibly get him down alive, though it was a perilous undertaking. Queer jobs sometimes fell to the lot of these attendants. When he finally reached him, he said quietly, "What's the matter with coming down?" And the patient answered, "Nothing." And he straightaway descended.

This boy's case was classified under what is called "Behaviorism," and this incident recalled to my mind one of these psychiatric reports I recently read. The boy, in the report, didn't get on well at school and was taken to a clinic where he was submitted to intelligence tests, emotional tests, tests of his reflexes and a thorough going through of his school and family history. Finally a physical examination revealed that he needed eyeglasses.

Our young tree-climbing friend was a problem boy all right and a very serious one. He was not yet twenty, but had already spent the greater part of his time since he was fifteen in prisons, hospitals, etc. The family was very well-to-do and able to endure almost any financial strain that would effect a cure. He was extraordinarily good-looking and judging from outside appearances, butter wouldn't melt in his mouth. He openly boasted that the institution wasn't built that it could hold him. I asked him how he managed to escape so often. He said it was easy. He usually got the attendant to take him for a long walk and when they were well out of sight of everybody, he just "knocked his unsuspecting victim flat with a blow to the chin." He was exceedingly powerful. At ten he had run off with a circus and there developed great strength in his muscles by acrobatic training. He was certainly hard as iron. Through it all he had preserved the speech, the manners, the outward appearance of a thoroughbred aristocrat. Well, I remarked, here's one place at least you can't break out. Three days later an alarm was sounded. He was missing. We never saw him again. Quite a chap—taking him all in all.

I didn't like these visiting days, as a general rule. They produced too many heartaches. When a patient is well on the road to recover, I think a call from family and friends is an excellent thing, and both sides seem to be the better for it, but I saw too many men strain their eyes, standing motionless, till certain figures faded from sight, and not a few let tears course down their cheeks. It's either that picture or the reverse—where curses are the only reward for a toilsome journey and bitter memories as a result.

In all great hospitals like ours, there are in constant circulation weird tales concerning this or that patient who is the center of some great tragedy or the leading figure in some sensational crime now being featured in all the great dailies. Quite naturally, a good many are registered under assumed names. The family's honor must be preserved from the stigma of insanity. That old fetish has marvelous tenacity. It seems impossible to kill it or remove it from the list of disgraceful performances. A few more centuries of progress at the present rate, and I honestly believe outside public opinion in this respect will change. Those in the inside have changed long ago.

So we pass many tedious hours, speculating whether that new patient in Ward Six is not really the ex-Crown Prince of Germany. His slanting chin and shifty eyes strongly resemble the familiar feature of this "nitwit" son of a "nitwit" father, or that rather good-looking man with a prominent lower lip is probably Alfonso who, having lost his throne, is now recovering from the shock. Mysterious whispers concerning a certain young woman on the other side drift to the men's quarters and we are told she is so rich that she is paying all our expenses out of sheer gratitude for the rest and relaxations she now enjoys.

Of the famous soldiers, statesmen, diplomats, world-wide literary celebrities, there is no end. It is a fertile field in which to exercise the rehabilitated imagination, and I always allowed my fancy to roam at will through this eerie domain. It did no harm to invest the scullery maid with the romance of royalty or the erstwhile bed chamber attendant with all the glamour of a temporarily dethroned movie queen.

There were, of course, many celebrities in our group besides myself, and I think it did us good to speculate upon their real identities. Not a few were genuine headliners.

happiness, it seems also to possess the opposite quality in equally magnificent proportions. Our friend, the green-eyed monster, is hand-maiden to love.

There was the case of a particularly bright chap who came into my ward just as I was about to receive my sheepskin. It again illustrates the fearful tragedies that lack of self-control provides. Sudden anger is hard to resist at times, and during the period when we are enjoying love's sweet dream it should be guarded against with the utmost vigor. That's a time when young people are particularly sensitive to a whole lot of things that we older people know are nonsensical.

The black misery of a lovers' quarrel is something we graybeards have forgotten about. Likewise, the exquisite bliss of "making up." I presume these two experiences are the Alpha and Omega of all human emotion, and the story I am about to relate is nothing unusual. The same thing happens every day and from the same sort of foolish cause. What lovers always wonder at, when they have made up, is why they could ever have been so foolish as to endure so much heartache for such a silly happening. Lovers have wondered at that for all time and probably always will.

Well, the young man I am speaking about had a quarrel with his sweetheart. She accused him of some slight of no earthly consequence; but, of course, he had to lose his temper, which in time caused her to do the same. No one ever seems to look ahead; no one ever seems to think of the disastrous consequences to which a silly few minutes of anger may lead. This young man could not even remember the details. "Just a sudden flare-up," he said, "over nothing."

They were both very fond of each other and were soon to be married. It was considered an ideal match.

He was sitting in the library one night, utterly wretched, when the phone rang. "Is it you?" said a soft voice he had been famished to hear. "Listen. I'm sorry. Pierre is here with the Packard. It does eighty. I will be home in half an hour. Run over."

He was immediately transported to dizzy heights of happiness. Fifteen minutes of the half hour passed. His car was outside to make the short run over to her house when the phone rang again. Grabbing it anxiously he heard:

"This is St. Luke's Hospital. A woman is here, badly injured—motor accident—and wants you to come quickly. Excuse me a second, the doctor wants to see me."

It seemed an age before he heard the voice again. Finally it said, "The doctor says, 'never mind,' she's dead."

He went raveling after that, and big game hunting. I'm afraid he also did a little drinking. I think I would have done some myself; not a little, but a great deal. Anyhow, he was with us and the doctors were doing their best to ward off permanent melancholia. Being young, they will succeed eventually, but it will take a long time. It's a bad thing to get angry over nothing; it's worse to get angry at all.

Notwithstanding the gloominess that surrounded my young friend who lost his fiancée so tragically, I liked him much better than another chap slightly older who was having a rather hard time. This young gentleman insisted on adding a member of Mrs. Warren's profession to the family circle and very properly the family objected. Now it is not for me to sit in judgment in a case of this kind, for I have known ladies of easy virtue to get married and make a huge success of it, and I have known men of the strictest probity to make a terrible mess of the same identical venture. Many of the noblest families of England have been physically enriched by the introduction of virile, fresh young blood from the musical comedy world and the stage, and that atmosphere is not regarded as the safest in which to rear a chaste but poor young maiden. If the family's objection had been based on pathological grounds and not moral, I think they would have succeeded in curing the young man's infatuation without having to throw him into the discard first. The doctors in our Hospital were quite well agreed that a woman of loose character is a pathological case, and that it is not a nice thing to introduce one of them into the family.

Even in my former life I came across one or two instances where young men were madly infatuated with women of this type, and I have known them to be pretty miserable when thwarted in their desire to marry them. It all reverts to self-control. If that had been observed in the first place, there would have been no subsequent complications. "I will live cleanly as a nobleman should," is often quoted, but to me it is an anachronism. I never knew any foreign nobleman to live cleanly, unless he was bankrupt or sick unto death. So Shakespeare's advice should be taken, in this instance, as merely a poetic license.

There are, of course, many legends in all hospitals concerning former noted patients. To the world they disappeared mysteriously, but after the customary nine days' wonder their existence was forgotten. Some rumor of death is put in circulation and never contradicted, and in due time this rumor becomes a fact, but by that time the patient has long ago been forgotten and his death occasions no comment.

This story concerns a woman well known in New York society. She now rests in Trinity Churchyard alongside the body of her husband whom she foully murdered almost sixty years ago. The circumstances surrounding the tragedy were known to but a few. It was pieced together by the police officials. Powerful influences were brought to bear at the time, and the story was never published, nor did she ever suffer for her crime, It was committed as the result of a terrible mistake. When the woman was restored to consciousness, her mind had left her completely. For almost half a century, she lived wholly unconscious of who she was, where she came from, or what brought her to the Hospital. Everybody connected with her admission had long ago disappeared. For many years she was to the attendants nothing but a severe case of mental maladjustment. At no time did she ever possess a single lucid moment in all those years. Even at her death there was none left who recalled the tragedy except as a tradition, and fortunately her passing away did not revive the story. Were it not that I afterwards looked up the facts, I would not now retell it. Even the man who made it possible for me to do so is among those who are no more.

In a sense, it is a pathological case; yet the result of an emotion so universal that I tell it as added emphasis to what is pointed out in almost every page of this book—the absolute necessity of self-control. None of us will deny the fact that jealousy is an emotion; nor that under stress of this particular emotion a vast number of crimes have been committed. It seems to be the one that stirs up the most devil in our natures. All the more need for its rigid suppression.

So this poor woman was a victim of this passion. One night her husband failed to appear for dinner, nor did he arrive to accompany her to the opera. She occupied their box alone, momentarily expecting his appearance. As the second act was about to begin, she was considerably startled, not to say shocked, to see him enter a box almost directly opposite accompanied by a strikingly beautiful woman—an entire stranger to the wife. When the opera was over, she hastened her carriage without waiting for her husband, or for him to present his fair companion.

Almost an hour passed before the husband returned to his home. A glass of wine and a slight repast awaited him.

"Drink your wine, dear," said his wife, "you look tired."

"Thank you, I will," he said, draining the glass. "You got my note all right, I see."

"What note? I received no message from you at all. Did you send me one? What was it about?"

"My sister, whom I haven't seen for years, arrived on the steamer today. I was amazed when I heard her voice over the phone. I wrote you a hasty note telling you of her arrival and not to wait dinner for me, that I would see her to her hotel and leave her with some friends at the opera. Why, what's the matter, dear?"

His wife had gone white. A moment later she swooned. She never came out of that swoon. In an hour the husband lay dead from the poison placed in his wine by the jealous wife.

Next to the philanderer, as a fool person, our doctors placed the "rummy."

The more I saw of mental sickness the more I was convinced that a large part of it could easily be avoided. One of the great sources of supply comes from a direction that many do not even suspect, yet a very common danger—very common indeed—is excessive drinking. The result of this pleasant pastime annually produces a large number of "rummies," as they were affectionately called in our Hospital. These social errors provide a considerable percentage in the census of every hospital.

I am not now speaking of the flop-house type—the utterly hopeless derelict, so far gone socially and spiritually as to be outside the pale of the present discussion. I am referring more especially to the "life of the party," who is in danger, but has yet abundant chances of escape.

I made the acquaintance of quite a number of these gentry during the scientific investigations I am now recording, and found them more or less interesting—generally less. These fascinating personages did not always arrive at the head of a noble procession preceded by a brass band. They frequently came unannounced, snugly ensconced in a costume of wool and canvas, securely laced at the back and sides, and accompanied by a varied assortment of pink elephants, flying horses, dancing swordfish and other flora and fauna of the hectic region which henceforth would know them no more. Their journey along the primrose path of dalliance was temporarily ended. Disinfectants and a powerful hose are now their portion and an iron cot their palace. It is hardly worth the price.

Now this is not what you would call an ideal experience. One would naturally imagine that after such a heartbreaking prelude, a "rummy," when restored to liberty would eschew John Barleycorn forever. Did they? Not from my observation. One of them, whose period was up, was to be released that afternoon. "By two o'clock," he informed me, "I will be on the Southwestern Limited. By three, I will be so beautifully corned that I won't know my own name or whether I'm coming or going. Oh! Boy!"

It is simply astonishing what a physical wreck a man can make of himself in a few weeks of steady drinking after he has come out of an institution in first-class physical shape. For months he has perforce lived an ideal life. His meals have been served him regularly on the dot. He has had regular, but not too exhausting, exercise. He has retired every night promptly at ten. A year of such living has made a new man of him. He probably thinks he can stand anything. Yet in two instances in our Hospital, liberty was followed by death soon after.

>>>>>>>>>>>>>>> Chapter Nine <<<<<<<<<<<<<<

Signs of My Returning Mind

In spite of all that was done for me, I remained, it seemed to me, about the same—no better, no worse. However, I was slowly but surely getting better.

How long I remained in the condition I have just described, I do not know—probably several months. Then I began to be more talkative. I mixed more with other patients, played checkers, ate checkers. I carried a checkerboard under my arm when we went outside for an airing. I played it with any one I could induce to join me. When I lost five or six games in succession, I would neatly arrange the board with all the men in their proper places for the next game. Then to the surprise of my partner, I would take a savage delight in kicking the whole thing skyward. I remember one game in particular when my opponent completely checked me in three moves. To show my admiration of his skill, I immediately swept the board clear, sending the checkers in every direction.

At first I played a stupid game, I wasn't interested in winning or losing. Then I really began to play to win, and did my best in every game. Unknown to myself, I was slowly but surely recovering the vital sense of interest. Ultimately, I became quite a skillful player, but I hope never again to see another checkerboard as long as I live.

The great objective of all psychiatry is to arouse that spirit of interest which is dormant in mental sickness, and it makes little difference how this interest is aroused or the medium by which it is accomplished. It may be checkers or John D.'s numerology, anything to bring back to life the dormant, natural impulse to do something. The first sign of this indicates that the inner consciousness is at last faintly stirring. How to fan this spark into a flame is now the problem.

I had not seen a book, a magazine, or paper for almost two years. I wrote letters, but not often. The ordinary pen of commerce contains suicidal potentialities and is therefore forbidden. Only pencils are available. In former days, I always disliked receiving a letter written in pencil; it seemed to me to exhibit a lack of respect or something. Anyhow, I hated writing with pencil so much that my writing was extremely limited, and although formerly a voluminous correspondent, I did not even remark this change in myself.

About this time there came to light one of those tragedies which are part of hospital life everywhere. This one moved me profoundly. It was really the first time my emotions had shown any sign of life in many months. I imagine I had been in the same state as is the boxer who has just received a blow on the button. For the time being, he is utterly indifferent to his surroundings, and a mental blow has much the same effect on the brain. In both cases, a knock-out has resulted. In the former, the injury is superficial, a dash of cold water curing the trouble. In the latter, the period of innocuous desuetude is more stubborn and the same remedy will not produce the same result. Something drastic is needed, and doubtless this event had the power to so affect me that long, slumbering faculty was at last restored to consciousness.

A certain patient had been here for many years. To me he seemed a pleasant, inoffensive sort of chap, well educated and apparently accustomed to the usages of polite society. He had been sick a long time—so long that only a few of the personnel of the Hospital anteceded his admission.

His was a curious case. The doctor diagnosed it as a Homicidal Mania. That is, he had his mind made up to kill a certain person if the chance ever presented itself. On all other matters, he was perfectly normal, and the doctor concluded that until that idea left his brain it was better that he stay where he was than decorate the chair at Sing Sing.

Finally the Hospital received word that the object of this man's wrath had passed on. How to acquaint the patient with this news, what effect it would have on this illness was now the problem. It was finally decided that no matter what happened the patient should be informed. He received the news with little or no emotion. Perhaps some shadow of a thought crossed his brain, but if the news meant anything to him, he gave no sign. That afternoon he fell into a quiet sleep while seated in a chair. The attendant wisely decided not to disturb him, though it was against the rules.

He slept well through the night, another unusual occurrence for him. After a shower and a good breakfast, he appeared to have changed very materially; yet his face still wore a strange expression, not dazed, but curious. Curiosity stuck out on every line and wrinkle. Finally he approached the charge nurse.

"Where am I?" he asked.

"In a hospital."

"Have I been sick?"

"Yes, you have been very sick."

"I thought so. When I looked in the glass this morning I seemed old and haggard. How long have I been ill?"

"A long time; but the doctor will be here in a moment. He will talk to you and tell you all about it. Won't you sit down?"

The doctor arrived and greeted the poor fellow with as much cordiality as the occasion permitted.

"Do you remember So and So?" he asked, when the greetings were over.

"So and So?" The man hesitated and a deep flush spread over his features. "Yes, I do, God damn him!"

"Don't say that," said the doctor. "He's dead, died on Monday, from a stroke."

Slowly the other seemed to grasp the significance of the statement. Finally he looked up. "I'm glad of that. He was a scoundrel if ever there was one. So he's dead, is he? I hope he's roasting in hell. Last Monday, was it? What's today?"

"Wednesday."

"Two days ago. So surely he's dead, is he? Well, that's good." And he left the doctor to go to his room.

In a few moments, the doctor joined him, knowing that the transmission gear of the brain had snapped back into position again and the cells were working.

"How long have I been here, Doctor? My folks must be worried. Did you send them word? I must go home right away? How is my wife?"

Gently, but kindly, the doctor told him that he had been sick a long time, a very long time.

"Months? Years?"

"Yes." Then he was told the years were over twenty.

"Is my wife well?"

"She's dead."

"And the children?"

"Gone too."

"All gone?"

"Yes."

He got up to look at himself and gazed long and anxiously at the deep lines in his face and the streaking gray hair. He resumed his seat quietly. "Guess I will think a bit." So the doctor left him.

In a few days he went away from the only home he had known

for almost half a lifetime. It was almost as if he had been born again.

When I finally became well enough to read with somewhat like my old accustomed avidity, I became more or less interested in what the other patients read. One of the forms of literary dissipation that was high in popular favor was crossword puzzles. In my normal days, I always looked upon this mental recreation as exclusively designed for morons. It requires, however, considerable concentration on the part of the patient, and to that extent was valuable. There was this great difference, however. The patient who put his time solving these puzzles made little or no improvement. The patient who took up *Science and Health*, for instance, did much better. From my observation I must admit that Mrs. Eddy's teachings attracted more followers and did a larger amount of good than those of any other writer.

The Bible trailed along a poor second. This result astounded me. I was never much impressed with Christian Science before, but when I saw what it could accomplish among a lot of mentally ill persons, I began to have a profound respect for it. Not a few patients attributed their recovery solely and unequivocally to the teachings of Mrs. Eddy. I studied this matter rather closely, but my conclusions did not alter my previous attitude to any great extent. I could not see that she had invented a new religion, but I did think she had adapted an old one to the modern manner. I think she has made the writings of the Synoptic Gospels much more intelligible to the present generation and has pruned the Bible of much that can be spared, after the plan of a gardener cutting a rose bush. A great many of her adherents place her on a par with Buddha, Mohammed, and Christ of Nazareth. It didn't seem to me to make much difference where they put her as long as her work helped those poor people around me. The Catholics did little Scripture reading, but quite a few were very devout in their attendance at Mass. Like most of the Protestants, they had little recourse to the printed Word of God. They seemed satisfied with whatever spiritual consolation was derived from attendance at divine service.

What other reading was done was confined largely to weeklies and monthlies. The Saturday publication of a Philadelphia concern, largely made up of fiction, had the largest audience. The others merely trailed along. The library had a most excellent assortment of good books, but did not make a pretense of supplying up-to-the-minute best sellers. For the most part, it contained the masterpieces of all the great classics, and I had a chance to read a great many works that I always meant to read but never had time to, like *Count of Monte Cristo*, *Moonstone*, *Dombey and Son*, *Lorna Doone*, and others. For the great part, however, I, like the vast majority of others, regaled myself with the works of Wallace, Fletcher, Oppenheim, Van Dine, Conan Doyle and other popular writers of that school. I skimmed through a great many of them. Occasionally one of them proved really interesting, but as a rule they did not hold the attention. Biography was different, and I greatly enjoyed the volumes of Edward Bok, giving his own life story and also that of his associate, Mr. Curtis. André Maurois' *Disraeli*, I thought very fine. I had been a great admirer of the English statesman during his lifetime and Mr. Maurois' work was superb. Ludwig's *Lincoln* surprised and delighted me. I could not understand how a foreigner could so completely grasp and interpret so vital an American as Lincoln. His volume gave me great pleasure.

This recovered interest in reading is one of the signs the doctors look for, and after its appearance is definitely permanent, it indicates a rapidly healing mind. When you once more become an omnivorous reader, your convalescence may be said to have made great strides and complete recovery is not far distant.

Metropolitan newspapers were distributed daily, but I never noticed that the day's doings attracted much comment among the patients. The items that attracted the most attention were those recounting the suicide of some poor devil by leaping from a window or jumping in front of a subway train; and such items as appeared from time to time dealing with the overcrowded conditions of State Hospitals. When the account of an escape appeared, none of us talked much about it, but when some dreadful tragedy resulted, as in the case of the man who drove his family to the edge of a cliff, threw them all over and then jumped himself, causing the death of six, it was passed over without comment. It was a knock-down argument against letting us out.

Card playing took up more time than reading. Contract seemed the most popular game. Poker seldom. Solitaire was much affected by one or two. Checkers by several. Pool had quite a few devotees and in the better wards billiards was really quite popular. I became quite proficient in the latter game and was easily champion among the patients. The only time I played with the champion among the nurses I beat him, too, but that, I imagine, was a fluke. I was rapidly getting well and my game improved with my health.

Chapter Ten

I Surprise The Doctors

I am now in the third year of my sojourn in "Heart's Desire." Within the past few days I have been greatly perturbed. I no longer try to avoid meeting my old friend, Life, as I walk down the road. In fact, we almost smiled at each other yesterday and tomorrow I fear I shall speak to her if her continued friendliness seems to invite such an advance. Strange that we, such warm friends always, should have quarreled so bitterly and all over nothing. She should have known I didn't mean what I said. She looked fine today.

The doctors are beginning to notice that a change has definitely arrived. I am more cheerful and considerably less of a blot on the landscape. I have even put a legend over my door in Greek letters, which arouses much curiosity. It was an idea borrowed from other and happier days. Its ironic application to the present appealed to me. I had once known a very charming lady in New York who pointed with great pride to a motto carved over the pretty lodge gates of her beautiful country estate. "I copied it from a lovely little villa I once saw while traveling in Greece," she told me. It read, "In this house we spend only hours of pleasure." My sweet friend's classical education had been sorely neglected, however, and she was in blissful ignorance that her idolized inscription was the sign manual of the oldest profession in the world. But that was the worsted motto I hung upon my wall.

I am now trying to trace, step by step, the things that finally led to my recovery and record the trifles that helped to steady the mind. I never had any delusions. Many business men that I knew imagined Napoleon must have looked like them. Some have little silver statuettes of him on horseback ornamenting their desks. I never was like that even on the outside and I was less so now.

I did not eat grass and think I was Man o' War. My stomach was not full of ten-penny nails, four-inch jack-screws, safety pins, collar buttons, copper wire, etc., as many others were, as shown by the prints in the X-ray rooms. If my mind was unhinged or physically impaired, as in *paresis*, I saw no evidence of it beyond a determination to do nothing but sit and mope. It's this sitting and moping business that constitutes the trouble in nervous breakdowns; how to dispel this morbidness is the great problem. There doesn't need to be physical illness. Nervous breakdowns flourish in a body free from disease. So in recording this rehabilitation period, it will be noted that the effort was directed along self-help lines and that arousing dormant interest was the chief end in view. There is no doubt that a desperate situation was met and overcome, but to locate the exact turning point, to assert positively that it was this or that precise thing, is difficult. This much I do know. I did not do it. My opinion is that it was done by the Grace of God, and the doctors.

Undoubtedly, an improved physical condition greatly helped. A long rest, regular, very regular, living; the total absence of the strenuous life, sent my weight up from 130 to 160, and later to 175. The doctors attach much importance to weight. If you persist in losing, you are taken in hand immediately and your diet is changed. If you gain, be it ever so little, that is a good sign. They claim that no mental advance can be made till the physical improvement appears. I don't know. Some of the worst cases are apparently in the pink physically. I was a tough customer, yet in no single instance did I ever attack an attendant with a real desire to do him bodily injury. I did, in sheer exasperation, chase a nurse out of the room occasionally, but that was simply to relieve some long pent-up emotion. I would be thinking of the precious time I was wasting, and become furious at my inability to do anything. Such an utterly useless existence! No wonder at times I wanted to jump out of my skin, and when some one appeared who personified my captivity, I just naturally wanted him out of my sight. Of course, the poor fellow, who had no intimation of my black thoughts, was naturally surprised to receive such a bellicose reception.

It was thoughts like these that produced my agitation; that compelled me to walk unceasingly and breathlessly all my waking hours.

If a normal man walked leisurely, for an hour, he would easily go a mile. The ordinary speed at which a man travels on a business errand is considerably greater than four miles an hour. I went at breakneck speed, I would say five miles an hour would be a conservative estimate. For over two years that condition prevailed and I was hard at the job—not eight hours, but nearer twelve. If you are fond of figures, you can multiply one day's record, at sixty miles, by seven hundred thirty, and you get the very respectable total of forty-three thousand eight hundred miles for my two years' performance. If you think these figures are too high, reduce them by half and you still have a formidable aggregate for a man nearing seventy and who could not sleep at night a single moment. Truly this human frame of ours is fearfully and wonderfully made. Only the superb care I had in the matter of feeding, bathing, egg-nogs and other material things, could preserve the physical body under such a frightful strain as I put upon it. Of course, I lost weight—in all, about fifty pounds at the extreme period. Looking back at this stage of my illness, I am still unable to see how I was ever able to stand on my feet. There must be a terrific reserve strength that we rarely put to the test. I have since heard some marvelous talks about this reserve strength. In all this time, days when I walked the swiftest and made the most distance, I experienced absolutely no sense of fatigue. With difficulty I kept myself in bed. Frequently I paced my room for hours, ceasing only for the moment when the night supervisor made his rounds, because I did not wish to be discovered. For those few moments I was apparently sound asleep in bed. When he passed the room, I was up and at it again. I think the whole thing was an amazing superhuman performance. To this day I cannot believe it really ever happened, but it did.

Under such circumstances, it was only natural that I did not read a newspaper or glance at a book—I, who enjoyed the same delicious intoxication from the mere music in the words of Shakespeare as another does the music of a great composer. I had shunned everything in literature as if it were a plague.

It is difficult now for me to fix an exact date when the reading habit once more asserted itself. It began, I remember, from a magazine article which attracted my attention one morning and which, after many heroic attempts, I finally succeeded in reading. It was a paper by Coolidge, shortly after returning to private life, describing his experience as President. The article itself did not appeal to me so much as the editor's achievement in capturing what was undoubtedly a prize in the publishing world. I was thrilled with the accomplishment rather than the story.

I knew something of the keen competition in this field and marveled at the editorial acumen which had achieved so brilliant a coup. What it awakened in me was a wild desire to get out and do something again, and that was of supreme importance in my struggle to recover. There was no reason why I shouldn't, I argued; this keeping me locked up was all sheer nonsense. I took that magazine to bed with me and tried hard to finish the article. I did not quite succeed at first, but gradually the sentences no longer danced across the page, and eventually I read the story through to the end. This, however, was not the work of one night. It took several but I finally acquired enough concentration and composure to read it through and understand it thoroughly. The doctors noted the incident and encouraged me to continue reading, and I fortunately happened upon another splendid story having the same quality, but this time in the story itself—the autobiography of Mrs. Mary Roberts Rinehart, familiar, no doubt, by this time to most of my readers. In it there was the same element of perseverance under difficulty and triumph over unheard of obstacles. And again that same chord within me was touched and I longed more than ever to get into action. I finally reached the conclusion that my desire was capable of accomplishment if I would only *act* instead of *thinking* all the time. So I concluded to do something, anything, that would replace star gazing by something practical and tangible in the direction of *action*.

In order to give this incident its proper background, I must go back a little, long before my hospital days, showing what in all probability brought the suggestion to mind.

In my old life I had acquired more or less diverting knowledge of Old New York, and on one or two occasions I had been asked to exhibit my store of treasures to sympathetic and understanding groups. To relieve the tedium of the long winter evenings in the Hospital, I now decided to organize what I called the Thursday Night Club, and to give some talks. At these meetings I acted as Chairman, Toastmaster, House Committee and also as Guest Speaker, when no other speaker volunteered.

As a rule, there were many interesting people in my impromptu audience. One young man told us of a thrilling escape from shipwreck off the Coast of California. He and his wife floated on top of a hatch-comb for twenty hours before being rescued. Another told of the wonderful contrivance upon which rest the huge buildings above the tracks of the New York Central which prevents vibration; another of an adventure with bandits in Italy; still another of the early mining days at Cripple Creek, and so on. I also managed to build up a quartette. I will admit that through the week they kept the rest of us on edge by their constant rehearsals, but that's a detail. They rendered "Old Jeffrey Amherst," "Harvard, Fair Harvard," and "Good Night, Ladies" with considerable snap and harmony. We also staged a burlesque on psychoanalysis, which was one of the funniest things I ever heard. The questions burned with satire and the answers were gorgeously hilarious.

The Thursday Night Club met with the hearty approval of the doctors and I was agreeably surprised when one of them remarked that the Hospital really felt indebted to me for this service. When I faintly suggested that they could easily repay the debt by letting me go, that lovely thought fell upon the floor with a dull, sickening thud. The advent of Spring put an end to the Thursday Night Club and another noble experiment passed into history.

But these talks, which I was obliged to give myself, when other speakers failed me, turned out to be a blessing in disguise to me, if not to the audience. They played an important part in my reconstruction days, by which I finally secured my discharge. The why and wherefore of this discharge is of more or less value to my story. It came about in this way.

A very good friend of mine in a nearby town concluded that these talks would be very acceptable to a group of men who lunched together once a week and usually had some prominent person to address them. As a rule, the average business man, as an after-dinner speaker, should, in the interests of common humanity, be suppressed. "We have with us this evening" has always sounded to me worse than any shrieking I have ever heard from the violent wards, but I digress. So he proposed that I lunch at his club and afterwards give them a little talk along the lines of the Thursday Night Club. That was all right with me. Anything to get out, even temporarily. I thought it wise, however, to stipulate that my friend should introduce me and that he should also have a substitute speaker in case I should blow up at the last moment. The doctors gave me permission to attend this affair.

When the fatal moment of introducing me arrived, it was my friend who "blew up." Sudden terror must have seized him upon the realization that he had asked a goof to address his club and he had failed to provide an emergency speaker! A few hasty words from me to the regular toastmaster supplied the necessary material for short introduction and a moment later I was on my feet.

"Before I begin," I said, "I would like to make sure that my voice can be heard in all parts of the room; because my stuff is good and I don't want you to miss any of it."

That modest beginning was well received, but I don't know whether they were laughing at the goof talking to them or at the joke. However, I went along until I reached the point where my friend was to kick my shin under the table as a signal that I had talked for ten minutes, but he got so interested in red flannel underwear, leg shows, Galway sluggers, the introduction of toilet paper, and other outstanding memoirs of the "Elegant Eighties," that he forgot all about it. And before I knew it a half hour had elapsed. In consternation I took my seat, rather abruptly.

What interested me most in this performance was, that I had faced the ordeal of my friend's collapse and the absence of a substitute speaker. These untoward happenings had not upset my equanimity in the least. On the way back to the Hospital I gave this rather strange experience very careful thought. I utterly failed to see wherein I was less normal than the men I had just met, few of whom could have faced situation as I did without more perturbation. These comforting reflections were rudely interrupted by my arrival at the Hospital. Less than an hour after leaving the festive board, I was again within the custody of the State.

Word of my performance had meanwhile percolated through

the walls of my prison, in the peculiar manner news has of reaching the subterranean world. The doctor spoke of it to me in the morning. I told him I had tried not to disgrace my Alma Mater and he was kind enough to assure me that everything had turned out well and I needn't worry.

Soon after I made an address on "Lincoln" before the same club. I had about four weeks to prepare this impromptu speech, and if I do say it myself, I made a very fair job of it.

That speech brought a request from the Board of Education to have it delivered at the High School. Here was a dilemma. None were conversant with my address and none knew the high station I occupied in the service of the State. The Board of Education kindly offered to send a car for me and also take me back. Worse and worse. I was anxious, of course, to enjoy another outing, but the Medical Staff declined the invitation with such unanimity and such wild enthusiasm that even I was susceptible to the fact that the idea had not been met with favor. So, in a roundabout way, word was conveyed to the humble Board that the gifted orator had a previous engagement on the day and at the hour that they had selected. Sorry.

I was beginning to enjoy the situation. Other invitations were received and permission granted to accept. Finally one came from the pet club of the head doctor himself. Three or four other medicos of the staff were also members.

I really enjoyed that session. The high and mighty autocrats of the Hospital occupied obscure seats with the common herd. I was on the dais on the right hand of the presiding officer, flanked on both sides by distinguished guests. For once in my life I enjoyed the introductory remarks that are usually so replete with fulsome flattering as to be embarrassing. The speaker couldn't say anything half good enough to suit me. I was quite willing to be compared to Aristotle, Socrates, Julius Caesar and Demosthenes. In fact, I thought they were all cheapskates compared to me. So they were, that day. Since then they have resumed their places of awe and majesty in my mind.

The speech, I think, was a success. At any rate, we laughed so much that I had to cut it short and there was a good deal of noise when I sat down. On my way out, I passed the doctors and contrived a snooty air designed to crush them. They refused to be crushed. They knew as well as I did that the lurking behind the palms was a demon in white duck who would clap me into a car and bear me back to the jungle, the moment I stuck my nose outside the door.

The events which I have just narrated did not, of course, occur within a few weeks or even months. Yet my first talk must have been made, I should think, about eighteen months after my arrival. It is hard to fix an exact date, but I was still in the Observation Ward where, as I said before, I spent a very long time, but I can positively identify the date of the article in the magazine, which was at the end of my third year. With the capacity to read an accomplished fact, I became a constant patron of the library. I always had a sneaking liking for mystery and detective stories, but in my normal days was rather ashamed of what I regarded as a plebeian taste. I now indulged it to the limit of my desires. I think I am indebted to Harry Leon Wilson for bringing back the first laugh I had enjoyed for many moons. *Ruggles of Red Gap* proved the talisman that opened that closed door. There was also one of those *Red Pepper* stories, popular twenty years ago, by Grace Richmond. I have forgotten the title. The little heroine possessed a vocabulary of surprising power and beauty. For a child of eleven, she was nothing short of marvelous. But, nevertheless, she was such a sweet character that I fell in love with her at once. I am not ashamed to admit that I laughed and cried with that little foundling, and I was sorry when she grew up and married a real nice and altogether splendid boy. I read that story more than once. I also took advantage of the opportunity to read some fiction that I always meant to read but never got around to. I fell desperately in love with Florence Dombey and my eyes were moist when I came to the death of little Paul, and the despair of the head of the house moved me deeply, though I did not like the character.

It may have been these early talks that made the doctors hesitate about sending me to the scrap-heap. The power to direct my thoughts into other channels and forget my troubles was long in coming; and took its place so quietly that I was long unaware of its presence. I guess that's the way the mind acts anyway. Evil thoughts come in the same manner. There ought to be a special dispensation of Providence to keep the rascals out.

Soon after the Lincoln speech, early in February, notice came to the charge nurse on my hall that I was to appear before the Medical Staff the next morning at 10:30.

I did. As I knew most of them more or less intimately by that time, we exchanged the usual morning courtesies. We were all chatting together when I was directed to take the chair. At these ceremonies you play the part of a star witness in Court. The doctors are the lawyers in this instance, and they begin to fire questions at you in rotation. One wants to know about this and another about that. Your replies which are carefully recorded are in due time added to your "history." It is from the general effect produced by this examination that the doctors decide whether you are well enough to be discharged or if a further detention is necessary. At this particular meeting there was no set examination. We seemed to fall into a natural conversation among ourselves, with no particular purpose in view. No technical questions were asked and no special remarks were made. I stood by the chair, but didn't sit down. The head doctor elevated his eyes a little, as if to invite questions from any one desiring to speak, but there was no response. After thanking me for my attendance, the meeting was over. In the course of a day or two I was asked what I would particularly like to do, and I said I would like to have all restrictions removed and to remain a week longer in order to give me time to pick up contact with the outside world and arrange for a place to live. This was at once granted.

So the doors of the Hospital once more clanged behind me. I joined Life, who was outside awaiting me, twirling a cane. Arm in arm we strolled down the road, singing gaily:

Many brave hearts are asleep in the deep—
To hell with a whole world lost!

>>>>>>>>>>>>>> Chapter Eleven <<<<<<<<<<<<<<

My First Day Out

I did not go directly to New York that day. It was very nice to be out in the world again and very much like Heaven to walk around and go where you wanted. Nobody unlocked a door for me when I went into a store, nor locked it after me when I came out. That seemed queer. I wondered if they were Martians. They were certainly creatures of another planet. They did not wear white duck and had no chains around their waists with a huge bunch of keys at the end. It was all very weird. I was quite puzzled to be greeted by several persons who were strangers to me, but who called me by name.

There was also an air of friendliness about the little town, which I liked, and as I had no special reason for going into the City, I concluded to remain where I was for the time being. When a storekeeper rang up a five-cent sale on the cash register, he said, "Thank you," instead of giving you a dirty look. The only thing that bothered me at first was the speed of the automobiles. One of them finally knocked me down, then chased me several blocks. They took me to a hospital, which hurt me more than the car did. I do not like hospitals. I remembered how in England, when they first began to use the public highways, a man had to precede a motor car on foot carrying a small red flag. I wish they would revive that ordinance; it would help to relieve the unemployment situation. A friend who took me riding the other day insisted on passing every car he met. Said he didn't like the smell of gasoline. I like the smell of gasoline better than that of iodoform, so I didn't go riding with him again.

It was awkward at first, paying for things as you got them, which I hadn't done for three years and only once or twice did I create a little excitement by walking out of a cigar store or restaurant without this necessary function, which was quickly excused when explanation was made. I had more trouble with my change than anything else, for I would leave it on the counter. Once I lost four dollars this way and it hurt. Another time, a man kept a dollar nearly a week for me, before I happened in again.

Other pleasant experiences occurred. A snapshot showing a team of oxen drawing a load of hay out on a country road was displayed in a sports shop window; a pastoral scene of rare charm and beauty, I thought, so I went in to buy it. The storekeeper said it was a private negative and not for sale. That made me want it all the more. So I wrote my name on a card asking the storekeeper to get permission from the owner to sell me a print. In a few days a beautiful enlargement came "with the compliments of the owner," but no name attached. It now hangs on my study wall and all my friends enjoy it with me.

So I was not sorry I stayed. Soon I was sailing along smoothly. It was quite an event when I began to call folks up on the telephone; jump into taxis and go to the pictures, all alone. It felt nice to be a regular guy once more.

It was early in May and the country was fascinating. A few moments' walk and you would be amidst almost virgin forests and green pastures. So I spent much time strolling along the rapidly disappearing dirt roads where the motor car was not.

In a few days I went to town and started contacts with old

associates, most of whom, as I have related, thought I had long ago died. New York looked nice; not so busy, except in spots, but to my eye much more stately and dignified. Many faces looked worried; one or two men talked to themselves as they walked along. Just like a hospital. And there were many new and higher buildings. Especially on Wall Street. In the evening, I wrote a letter to the editor of a popular magazine, thanking him for his unconscious assistance in getting me out of the jungle. His response was a telephone message asking me to call. When he heard me talk, he said, "Write it." So I sold him a story for which he paid me a lot more money than it was worth, and I felt that I was once again part of our workaday world.

Soon after my leaving the Hospital my medical advisers decided that I should have an entire change of environment and a complete new world to live in for a period. I packed my trunk and set sail for Europe. I had never had a chance to see the great cities of the world and welcomed this suggestion with open arms. There was so much to see and so much to marvel at that there was no room left for old and hateful memories. I was particularly interested in the cities and places connected with the history of New York. I especially enjoyed my visit to old York in England, from which New York got its name. York still has so many Roman ruins that it almost rivals in interest the Eternal City itself. It is said to have been founded by a near relative of that greatest of all psalmists, David, the sweet singer of Israel, but I think it was made by the angels. In the Town Hall I was shown the brass memorial tablet presented by the City of New York on the occasion of its three hundredth birthday, to its namesake, and it seemed a gracious thing to have done.

On the Continent I was particularly interested in the little Town of Gheel in Belgium, that marvelous retreat for the mentally ill. The night before I reached it, I stayed at that famous little Belgian town, Waterloo. That was a delightful and enjoyable experience. It was raining when I took the trolley from Brussels in the late afternoon, intending to stay overnight and see the Battlefield in the morning. The conductor let me off in front of an old church; opposite I saw an old tavern bearing a sign "Wellington's Headquarters." I entered, and after dinner I asked the proprietor if this was really where the Iron Duke stayed. "Yes," he answered, "Come upstairs and I'll show you his room, his little iron cot, and the lamp and table he used when dictating dispatches. They are all just as he left them."

"I would like to occupy that room tonight myself," I said, on the way upstairs, "if you don't mind."

"Not at all. You're very welcome, if you like it."

But alas! There was no mattress on the cot, no pillows and no blankets, so I did the next best thing and took the adjoining room.

The next day I went to the Farm Caillot where Napoleon spent the night during the great battle. It is now a miniature Napoleonic Museum. A bronze tablet affixed to the foot of the bed, records the three-day stay of the Emperor. In the afternoon, I visited the orchard where Napoleon, a fugitive and all alone, spent an hour in bitter reflection ere he was taken prisoner. What emotions must have been his in that brief period when the god shrank into the man! A beautiful bronze monument marks the spot where the last charge of the Old Guard was made. The design is a huge eagle, with an arrow shot through its heart, and you almost feel its death throes as you gaze upon its dying agony.

Gheel is a green oasis of the crofters' cottages in a wide sea of sand called the Campine. The streets of Gheel, worn for a thousand years by the footsteps of unhappy pilgrims, are now visited by the philanthropic investigators of all lands who study the most merciful ways of treating the most pitiable of human afflictions. The experiment of the Belgian Government, at first held to be perilous, has proved as successful as its purpose was beneficent. Her insane poor are cared for by giving them the freedom of the open air and the fields, and placing them in small boarding houses in the wide open sea-cooled country, under sympathetic supervision. All about them are rippling linden trees and ever-turning castle-like windmills. A prince who sought refuge at Gheel said, "I am a little deranged, but the *quiet* here helps me." The quiet is atmospheric—it can be felt, it is hypnotic and brings healing in its wings. Nor is it the quiet of the air, the fields, the gardens and linden trees, but of the hope in all faces. The afflicted people are sent there to recover and many of them do, or come to have a more hopeful, pleasanter imagination. Call it hypnotism, superstition, or whatever you will, and there is no experience in life so hard or so sad that one may not glorify it by noble sympathy.

The houses are old, the streets clean, and over all looms the great Church of Ste. Dymphna—patron saint of the insane. Gheel is a commune—a kindergarten for those who have become children again. It leads the imagination into the free air and fields. One recalls the old conditions that have prevailed, and unfortunately still prevail in some parts of our country, of tying to bedposts and staples those whose wills became weak and nerves unbalanced, of such as rattled their chains on the approach of friends and whose cries and moans made wakeful nights in lonely houses until merciful death brought the blessing of silence; of suicides who, on account of their so-called "self-murder," were buried in lots apart from the common villages of the dead and upon whose graves the ignorant cast stones with looks of terror. The Catholic Church still persists in this uncharitable attitude toward suicides and it ought to be ashamed of itself. No man commits suicide in his right senses. Al Smith, who has done more for the mentally ill in New York than almost anyone else, should put a flea in Cardinal Hayes' ear on this subject. Some of our Southern States still confine patients in iron cages like wild animals in the zoo, but with none of the care bestowed on the latter in the way of good food, proper sanitation, and physical care, and that isn't to our credit.

The miracle-like achievements at Gheel are not the results of hypnotism or any other "ism." It is the natural operation of sympathetic faith in human nature plus a practical plan whereby its best results can be realized. Here is a community that for centuries has been brought up in an atmosphere of sympathy and kindliness for the unfortunates in this village. To them there comes no specter of a human form possessed of a devil because a person rambles in speech or hesitates at a street crossing. They do not think or speak of queerness.

The most important building in this town is the really beautiful Cathedral of Ste. Dymphna. It has a great crucifix hanging from the arch over the imposing and beautiful altar; there are fine carvings of the Stations of the Cross; the pulpit is upheld by divine little cherubs; and above all is a beautiful colored statue of Princess Dymphna. Outside, on the highway leading to the church, is a group of figures depicting the death of the Princess whose father was an ancient King of Ireland and who had her beheaded for her kindness to the insane. At her death, deranged people were said to have been restored to health and this shrine was erected to commemorate this miraculous healing. This is now the beautiful Church of Ste. Dymphna, a place of prayer for the recovery of the insane, and is full of beautiful legendary lore concerning its miracles of the past. The Tomb of Ste. Dymphna has become a place of pilgrimages for the healing of deranged folk. The written records of the Commune, or hospital as we would call it, do not go beyond 1300, but there are desultory fragments of papers, etc., extending back to about 600 A.D. The town is literally steeped in legendary lore and the strangest thing about it all is that in spite of all that may be offered in the way of criticism of this harmless lore, the fact remains that most of the patients become harmless there. The work of the hospital continues to be one of the most successful experiments in mental healing that has ever been made.

No doubt hypnotism plays a part. Gheel makes for the patients a new imagination. The dark despair that seemed hopeless at first gradually gives way to a more hopeful spirit. Disturbed patients believe they will calm down once they get to Gheel. The strange fact remains that they really do calm down. And it's the new imagination that effects this wonderful change.

Along the main street one passes strange dog carts on which three dogs do the work of a horse. These carts are gradually disappearing, but still lend an attraction to the town. The peasants peddle their milk and vegetables in them and the patients use them as we do buses. The *nourriciers*, or farm people who look after the patients, are under the direction of a medical inspector. It is a business to which they have long been accustomed, as the same families have followed the profession for generation after generation. No scoldings, imprecations or fault-finding is permitted. Most patients feel that they are being horribly persecuted; but the farm people have been taught to control themselves no matter what irritating things are said to them and never reply in kind. Nagging is an offense sure to bring swift condemnation from the inspector. It is practically unknown.

I have been asked to analyze just exactly the process by which my mind recovered from its state of apparently hopeless depression. That is hard to describe. Looking backward I am conscious of no one symptom or sensation that I could say marked the beginning of the end. Just as one does not fall into this state in a moment, neither does one come out of it in a moment. I remember discussing the matter with Dr. Bleuler during the visit to which I have already referred. When he told me I would surely get well, I said, "When?"

That he could not say. "You are no longer young," he answered, "and recovery will be slower on that account, but you need have no fear; you will ultimately be well and sooner than you expect." That seemed poor consolation, but his young son seemed highly elated. "Father knows more about this trouble than any one else in the world," he said, with pardonable pride, when we were alone again, "and I am tremendously happy for your sake; Father never makes a mistake."

I recalled this conversation some years later when I read the sad story of Nijinski's breakdown. Mrs. Nijinski took him to Dr. Bleuler. You will read in her book how the doctor told her as gently as he could that his case was hopeless and that while everything would be done for him that could be done, she had a duty to perform to the living as to the dead and she must consider her husband as having passed away and turn her thought to the care of her other responsibilities.

I have also a sad memory, as well as a happy one, of that visit. This promising young son of Dr. Bleuler left soon after to spend his summer holiday in Switzerland. He was in his early twenties, had just graduated from college with high honors, and life certainly held out great promise for a distinguished career. But on this vacation, while on one of those fool climbing trips in the Alps, he slipped and fell. His neck was broken. He was not killed outright, and now wears an iron mask to support the head on its useless neck. There is no cure for such an injury and he must go through life with this dreadful maiming. One is sorely tempted at times to doubt that "He doeth all things well," but it is not for us to judge. When the news of this dreadful accident reached me, I couldn't help feeling that a useful life was sacrificed and a useless one preserved.

I cannot say that I shared in the elation of the young doctor over his father's favorable prophecy. These dark shadows do not disappear like a sun breaking through the clouds. The change is so gradual, so imperceptible, that it cannot be noticed from day to day. Fear still holds you back, and that must be conquered. Even if you do get well, what are you going to do with yourself? Nobody wants a man your age, so what's the use? You're through! But after a while you begin to think you might do something. Anyhow you could always carry a sign in the Salvation Army, "A man may be Down, but he's never Out," or you could dress yourself up as Santa Claus and stand on the corner ringing a bell during the merry Yuletide season. Such reflections had their uses. It showed that the old bean was beginning to work again, and the fact that I could laugh at the scenes I depicted, was such a relief that I encouraged my mind to go further along this primrose path of dalliance. If I was in the Land of Make Believe, why not make it a pleasant land? Why let it continue to be peopled by Attila and his Huns when you might as well have Ariel and her blithesome spirits? I had gotten nowhere in my orgy of despair; a change could do no harm and it might do good. This was not easy. It was like starting to climb a steep hill and you had to force yourself to do it. Any mental exertion at this stage seemed impossible. Yet, if you were ever to get out of the darkness into light, you had to make a beginning. The power of concentration had to be employed. No one could help you do that; it was strictly your own job. The doctors were doing all they could, but the real cure must come from within and from *yourself.* Surgery can do almost miracles these days, but mental illness is vastly different from physical; so relief from that source was out of the question.

These thoughts kept running through my head constantly and instead of feeling exhausted after each tussle with myself, as happened at first, usually winding up with "Oh! hell, what's the use," I began to consider the possibility of this new idea. It might be good; it could not possibly do harm. I stuck my teeth in the task and determined to try the new deal at all hazards. It was far from easy at first. The power to forget the past is not easy. Time and time alone can do that. My wounds were still raw, but thinking of the past only served to prevent their healing and that must be stopped, come what may.

Under normal conditions the mind in time will forget any great sorrow or unhappy catastrophe, but it is not accomplished in a day, or a month, or a year. Yet it will ultimately be forgotten. That's a wise and beneficent provision of Nature.

A new lease on life now began for me. I can't say that I was wildly enthusiastic about it. The prospect was far from alluring, but the struggle for existence had to be faced. I was fearful of the results that might follow the publication of my story in the magazine, which would soon appear, and in which I had told briefly the story of my hospital life. One does not usually advertise to the world that one has been insane, and what the effect would be in my case, I could only surmise.

I am happy to state that it was received by the public in a generous spirit. In it I frankly discussed my desperate situation and admitted that this was an attempt to stage a "comeback." I was at heart fearful of the result, but when letters came in from all parts of the country commending me for having the courage to discuss such a tragic experience, I felt much relieved. I was especially pleased with the fact that I had apparently robbed so-called "insanity" of much of its former terror and proved conclusively that it was a sickness that could be cured and not something supernatural and the exclusive product of the Prince of Darkness. It seemed to have given fresh hope and renewed strength to many on the edge of despair, who would soon have given up. These letters moved me greatly. I answered each one personally, though it was a prodigious task. I felt that the least I could do was to show that I appreciated their kindness and interest in me.

The letters which discussed personal cases, for the most part told only half-truths. In one case where a woman confessed that she was beginning to drink rather heavily, I think I could have written her something that might have caused her to stop that foolishness, but unfortunately she signed her letter with only her initials and, of course, a reply could not reach her. I asked the postmaster to make a special effort and told him why, but it was a large city and he failed. That was some months ago, and though she will doubtless read this book, a year of such a delightfully progressive habit is a very considerable period and her powers of resistance may have been greatly weakened in the meantime. From a prison, a convict wrote me in a spirit of camaraderie, hailing me as a friend and a brother, because we both knew what it was to be locked up. I answered in the same friendly fashion, calling him a lucky stiff not to have lost his health; and wishing him well. When he gets out we will go blotto together, ring doorbells and kiss the hostess.

Except in a few isolated instances, I have experienced no change in the attitude of my old friends. Shortly before my magazine article appeared, I made the acquaintance of a charming couple who seemed likely to be numbered among the friends I could count on, in my new life, but that was not to be. After the story came out, a luncheon engagement was postponed. A trivial excuse was offered and accepted as a matter of course, but our intimacy ceased. From that day to this, my erstwhile admirers have stayed out of the picture. By a heroic effort I have managed to survive this ghastly incident.

Judging from my experience, I should say that no one has anything to fear socially from the result of a nervous breakdown. There may be one or two isolated instances such as I have noted, but on the whole there is no change. What change there is I can truthfully say is for the better. Many persons are drawn to you as a result of sympathetic understanding, and life is richer. There seems to be a better outlook and a wider horizon as a recompense for the suffering one has undergone.

I was very careful, however, in answering these letters. I never interfered on the medical side or gave any suggestions as to treatment. That was entirely a matter for the family doctor. I devoted my attention wholly to comforting the correspondents who were suffering almost as much as the patient. In some instances, that suffering was so intense that it was bound to have disastrous results if some effort was not made to counteract the gloomy thoughts that were heading them straight to a depression. And there were many callers.

Early one Sunday morning, when I was still deep in my beauty sleep, the phone rang. A lady and her daughter had come all the way from Rochester to see me and asked if I would honor them by taking breakfast with them. I said I would and an hour later was seated with them at their hotel. It would be hard to find a more dejected, utterly wretched couple. They made the beautiful dining room look like a funeral parlor.

"The first thing I am going to ask you ladies to do," I said, after listening to their profuse apologies for disturbing me so early, "is to smile. You've brought enough gloom with you to sink a ship." Their faces brightened perceptibly, and in a few minutes they were listening intently to some diverting story I introduced.

Breakfast over I said: "Now let's get down to business. One of your men folks has been sent to an institution and you are desperately worried. You think I can help. So I can, but you must promise to take my prescription three times a day."

This frank approach established at once a feeling of friendly confidence and soon the story was told. The boy was about twenty-one, had become violent, and had to be put away. They had just been to see him, and he had regaled them with terrible tales about how frightfully he was treated and the cruelty that was practiced upon him. It happened to be the same institution where I had sojourned, so I knew all about the conditions he would be called upon to face.

"He struck some of the attendants, didn't he?"

"Yes."

"Well, he knew perfectly well what he was doing, but he didn't care to restrain himself. He's now where he has *got* to restrain himself, and it will do him good. If he had learned to control himself earlier, the chances are that he wouldn't be where he is now. Was he disciplined much at home?"

"No. That's the trouble. We always let him have his own way."

"Exactly. Now he must receive the discipline that you neglected. Attendants don't kiss an unruly patient to make him behave, neither do they unnecessarily hurt him. In that particular hospital there are fortunately more men than one to handle an outburst of that kind. Consequently, the patient is subdued before he can do much harm to the attendant or to himself. He will learn that he can't punish people with impunity—something which he has temporarily forgotten. When his anger cools off, he will understand that it is better to be nice than nasty, and the lessons will benefit him tremendously. They don't abuse patients up there. They correct their behavior when necessary, but no attendant dare strike a patient on pain of instant dismissal, as it is against the law."

"But my boy says they almost twisted his arms off and nearly broke his back."

"Did you detect any symptoms of serious injury?"

"W-e-l-l, no."

"That's because there weren't any. He was probably jujitsued and otherwise experienced the rather rough handling which he invited by attacking the attendant. He was overpowered long before he could do any damage to the keeper, thus inviting severe reprisal, or to himself, which is equally disastrous. Don't worry. What he got will help him control his temper next time he feels like striking any one."

This reasonable attitude deeply impressed my visitors. Evidently they had had similar experiences at home and were secretly glad that the corrective measures were administered so promptly and so efficaciously.

So the conversation drifted along to other channels. I explained that she could rely on my statement that the illness was positively only temporary. I was there in the flesh to prove the correctness of my contention and that was evidence which she could not disprove. So she suddenly seemed to have dropped off a heavy load, the rest of our talk being in a very cheerful vein. My new-found friend was loud in her praises of the relief I had brought to her mind, which I was glad to hear.

I have rarely seen two women change so much in so short a time, and it was all the result of a change in their own minds. They replaced horror and despair with hope and cheerfulness. I made no motion to go till I was sure that this altered attitude would last, and the grateful words those women uttered when we finally parted, more than repaid me for the time I gave them.

Some very fine friendships have resulted from these calls. All are not concerned with their own troubles. Not a few are from persons who drop in merely to say, "How are you?" and to wish me Godspeed. Life evidently has its compensations no matter what the circumstances.

Each caller demands different treatment. Some are determined that no one could possibly suffer as much as they. In that case, I would cite instances of trouble much greater than theirs, which had been met and conquered by others. Also of what seemed impossible—good coming out of evil. To illustrate this, I told a story which I had heard as a boy from my father.

My dad was a Scotchman, and the scene of this story was laid on the border line between that country and England in days of old when knights were bold.

Money was not plentiful in those times and when the chieftains on either side were hungry and had no money, they used to gather together some of their clan and raid a farm on either side of the border, particularly where a herd of fat beef cattle could be driven off. It was understood on both sides that if one or the other were unsuccessful in the raid and taken prisoner, they were to be hanged by the neck till they were dead. With this fair and kindly understanding the marauding went merrily on, for the clans were always hungry and never had any money. This added much color to an otherwise drab existence. So between hanging and stealing, a good time was had by all.

Now when the Lord denies a women beauty, he generally makes it up to her in irresistible sweetness of soul and fascinating brightness of mind.

In accordance with this custom, a young chief, wanting beef as usual, made a raid on his border neighbor who owned a splendid herd of cattle and proceeded to drive off a goodly number to his own land, but the old fellow was on the lookout. He mustered his clan and gave battle to the marauders, beat them, took the young chief prisoner, locked him in the dungeon, and then went home very much delighted and highly pleased with himself.

Arriving there, his wife heard the story and asked: "Noo, my man, what are you goin' to do with the prisoner?"

"I am goin' to hang him" the old man thundered, "just as soon as I've had my dinner."

"But I think ye're naw wise to do that," she ventured, "he's got a fine place, ye ken, ower the border, and he's a braw young fellow himsel'. Now I tell ye what I'd do. I would give him his chance to be hung or marry oor Meg."

Now Meg, the chieftain's daughter was one of these unlovely lovely creatures who seemed likely to become one of these domestic tragedies—an uncalled-for treasure. So the wife's suggestion appealed to the old warrior and he agreed to try the plan. After eating, he repaired to the dungeon.

He told the young chief to get ready to be hung in half an hour. After letting that pleasant thought sink in a good ten minutes, he then got round to the alternative proposition; that he would spare his life if he would marry his daughter Meg and throw the steers into the bargain.

The young chief had heard of Meg's wonderful want of beauty, and so with native canniness he said, "Ye will no mind, laird, letting me see my intended before I make up my mind, wud ye? Because maybe I'd rather be hung."

"Aye mon, that's only fair," the old chief answered and went in to bid the mother get Meg ready for the coming of her lover.

The mother did her best to make Meg attractive and winsome, but when the swain saw the object of his involuntary devotion, he weakened and said to the old chief: "Laird, if ye has no objection, I'd rather be hung."

"And ye shall, and welcome," roared out the old warrior, wild with rage.

So they led him out, got the rope round his neck, and then the young man changed his mind. He was only twenty-one and life was very sweet. "Laird, I'll take her," he yelled just before the noose choked off further speech.

So he was marched back into the castle, married forewith. Tradition has it that there never was a happier pair in Scotland, and never a better wife in the world than Meg. Everybody loved her.

Meg's main detraction was her very large mouth, and now in the direct line in almost every generation that mouth reappears. When it does the neighbors and friends are delighted and cry with joy: "Here's Meg back again. Glory be!" Sir Walter Scott was one of Meg's descendants and inherited Meg's famous mouth. "That's why I was so warmly welcomed," he would say as he related the story with great glee.

But the best part of this story is the sequel. Years after Meg died, they found in a secret drawer of her old desk of sheet of paper closely written. It was hard to decipher, but Sir Walter finally succeeded. It was Meg's account of her wedding, not as it really was, but as it should have been according to Meg's idea. Her beautiful married life; the unending happiness that had been hers and the loving kindness of her brave but marauding lover should have had, according to Meg's ideas, a more romantic beginning. Sir Walter sensed the beautiful and poetic spirit that was in the thoughts of Meg. So he sat down and gave expression to the words in the heart of Meg, but which she had not the genius to put on paper, and if you will read *Young Lochinvar,* you will see what he wrote.

This story always produced a wonderful effect. It proved that what seemed a tragedy might easily turn out to be a blessing in disguise. Men and women who came to me almost beside themselves in an agony of fear, were strangely comforted The futility of the worrying—the absolute uselessness of constantly fretting—seemed all at once to make itself manifest. The duty they owed to the living, which they naturally were neglecting, appeared in a wholly new and vibrant aspect. The children, the home that was slowly but surely losing its sweetness and light, became once more a dominant note in their lives. They took up their crosses, determined to wage a conquering battle, come what may, and henceforth to live one day at a time. It was not impossible that their own hard trial would likewise have a happy ending.

Perhaps I am taking up too much of your time relating thus in detail the events that made up the first weeks of my new freedom, but there may be a more than passing interest watching the unfolding of a dormant mind, the gradual resumption of life after a practical death of three years. To me every sensation was new and enjoyable.

When a man has spent three years in close and intimate contact with what we call in the vernacular "nuts," he begins to study what this curious thing is we call a mind; to wonder what sort of an ancestry the mind has, if any, and why it is that it seems so easy to shove it over the border line of order into chaos. When you begin to investigate the past history of the race and its development, you are not so greatly surprised after all at its frailty, especially when one recalls the age long period of idolatry and superstition under which this poor old world of ours existed. One is compelled to admit that we haven't such a wonderful ancestry mentally as we fondly imagined.

For centuries we dwelt in semi-darkness and worshiped all manner of strange and fearsome things. Our gods and rulers were the progeny of mythological figures. Cybele, Attis, Endymion, Egeria, King Nemi, Diana, and Virbius are only a few of our early ancestors.

>>>>>>>>>>>>>>> Chapter Twelve <<<<<<<<<<<<<<

"Take It From Me—"

Years ago this country was the happy hunting round of more fakirs, charlatans and humbugs in the line of Gypsy fortune tellers, palm readers, astrologers and other variants of the get-rich-quick school of philandering, than one can readily believe. The papers unblushingly carried huge advertisements of their offerings and recitals of their wonderful predictions of recent events which they had accurately foretold weeks before. Lost lovers would be restored, domestic rifts would be healed, vast fortunes made overnight in Wall Street, and deadly diseases cured at once. Fee 50 cents. It was simply astonishing the amount of money these people wheedled out of the simple-minded morons who comprise such a large portion of any community. The only thing these sooth-sayers failed to do was predict their own upcoming annihilation. The spies, sent by the Detective Bureau of the Police Department to get evidence against them, had no trouble at all. "I see a tall, handsome, dark man in the distance gazing fondly at you," the seer would read from the palm of the woman detective's hand, "but it will cost you another dollar to know if he bodes evil or good." There was a tall, handsome man in the distance all right, if you will admit that all detectives are "tall and handsome," but these spirit rappers hadn't the slightest idea they were telling the truth for once, so many of them landed in jail.

But these picturesque and amusing gentry are virtually harmless compared with the vast army of charlatans professing to be psychiatrists. The very name is one to conjure with, it sounds so impressive, so mysterious—almost hair-raising. And it is a science so little understood by the best of them that it is attracting a constantly increasing number of quacks in every city, relying on the comparatively slim chance of discovery. For one thing, they need not prescribe drugs except to those patients who must be drugged or feel that they haven't had their money's worth. They prescribe a harmless cathartic taken once a day in a glass of aqua pura and get action which satisfies the patient without exposing their own ignorance of medicine.

But, how are you going to tell the sheep from the goats? Their offices all look alike. The waiting room has the same popular periodicals and the same group of hectic patients waiting to see the doctor. Inside the evidence multiplies that you are in the right place. The glass-topped desk with the French telephone resting conveniently at the great man's elbow; the private examination room with its scales, blood pressure impedimenta, ultra-violet ray lamps, metabolism headpiece, etc., are all present and accounted for. Even important people are brusquely spoken to by the doctor who is annoyed (?) at the interruption. The stage setting is perfect; the deception is complete. I know one woman who has been in the hands of one of those charlatans for seven years and has spent nearly a hundred thousand dollars. She is not one bit better now than when she began, and what is more, never will be under his ministrations. However, it's her money to spend as she chooses, and she thinks he is doing her good. So he is, but not in the sense she understands it.

Your own reliable family physician is the only one whom you should consult when you feel something is wrong. When you are finally satisfied that the trouble is something not *physical*, you naturally won't think it a matter for consultation with your regular doctor, who may not claim to be a nerve specialist. That is exactly where you make a great mistake. Every doctor knows the symptoms of a neurotic condition, and if he is your old family friend, who has treated you for years, he will be the first to tell you that he is not competent to treat your case (if he reaches that decision) and will gladly put you in the hands of one who is.

His advice is the only one to take. Never mind if Mrs. So and So, who goes to that Hindu doctor, is ever so much better lately. Leave these imported Gandhis alone and stick to the domestic article. If not, you will surely get into serious trouble. Above all things, you need to be absolutely convinced that there is nothing serious the matter with you, and that feeling will come only from one in whom you repose confidence. You will always have misgivings dealing with a strange doctor.

There is another safe way of getting the right advice. Have some male member of the family write to the nearest State Hospital for an appointment to talk the matter over with their head medical director. At that interview, you should come prepared with a history of your case prepared by your own doctor. That puts the state medical man directly at his ease. He knows that the other doctor understands your case and will correctly describe the situation to him. Upon reading this history, the state doctor can quite accurately judge the seriousness of the case. If it is not one requiring confinement, he can send you to a reputable psychiatrist in your vicinity, capable of handling the situation. He will not recommend confinement unless it is absolutely imperative and necessary for the safety of the patient himself, as well as for others.

To this advice regarding the proper selection of a doctor, I would like to add another word of caution about these many pamphlets that find their way into print, purporting to convey the very latest deductions and conclusions reached by so-called "expert diagnosticians" in the field of psychiatry. Don't take them to seriously. They are not so dreadful as they seem. Most of these reports are issued by well-meaning organizations of excellent reputation; more's the pity. They are absolutely sincere in their endeavors to promote a wider knowledge of this scientific problem, but this research work must necessarily be done by staff members, many of whom have little else to recommend them besides their enthusiasm for their work.

A critical analysis pointing out supposed elements of cruelty, anxiety, danger, and destruction in Lewis Carroll's "Alice's Adventures in Wonderland" and casting serious doubts that the book should be read by children, was placed before the annual meeting of the American Psychoanalytic Association recently at the Waldorf-Astoria, by Dr. Paul Schilder, of the Psychiatric Division of Bellevue Hospital and Research Professor in the Medical College of New York University.

As a perfect specimen of the utter tosh which many psychiatrists see fit to unloose on a credulous world, this particular paper is entitled to high rank. It would be difficult to include, in the same number of words on any subject, as much puerile nonsense and absolute drivel as this learned professor has managed to cram into his short address. He prefaced his remarks by a wholly unnecessary sinister allusion to Carroll, whose real name, he informed his gaping audience, (as if the whole world didn't know it), was not Lewis Carroll at all, but the Reverend Charles Lutwidge Dodgson. He claimed that as a child Carroll had amused himself with snails and toads as pets and had endowed earthworms with pieces of pipe so that they could make better warfare. He didn't explain how the latter was accomplished, however. He also pillories Carroll "because he was a mathematician and stammered," adding "it may be that ruthlessness toward space and time belong to the characteristics of mathematical talent."

There is no historical basis for this malicious statement

concerning Carroll's adolescent days and while stammering is an affliction and one that calls for sympathy, it has no connection with ruthlessness. England's new monarch, George VI, is one of the most kindly and lovable men and also one of the worst stammerers.

But let us consider further the fulminations of this amazing professor who finds this book to contain "preponderant oral sadistic trends of cannibalistic character."

"Alice does not get anything at the mad tea party," he says. "The oral aggressiveness is found everywhere. The poem of 'The Walrus and the Carpenter' is of an astonishing cruelty. The Lobster is cooked. Alice herself frightens the Mouse and the Birds by tales of devouring. There is also an owl to be devoured by a panther. The Crocodile devours the little fish."

Then Dr. Schilder took up the instances of "cruelty" which he found in the book.

"The Queen of Hearts wants to chop off everybody's head," he cried. "There is a serious discussion whether one can cut off the head of the Cheshire Cat when the head appears alone. It is the fear of being cut to pieces which comes again and again into the foreground. The head of the Jabberwock is cut off, too. The Prisoner (the messenger) is threatened with death, as is the Knave of Hearts. Thus there is a continuous threat to the integrity of the body in general."

The psychiatrist was concerned also with the manner in which Carroll continually threatened the stability of space, a condition which he said was normally "guaranteed by the vestibular apparatus and by postural reflexes." If anybody on earth, or out of it, can tell us what is meant by a condition which is normally "guaranteed by the vestibular apparatus and by postural reflexes," we would be profoundly grateful. A world peopled by little children after the pattern of Dr. Schilder might be an improvement over the children in Lewis Carroll's world and then again it might not, but please excuse us from inhabiting the same sphere with them.

Upon recalling that the Walrus and the Carpenter go out in sunshine when it is night; that the White Knight carries a little box upside down so that the rain cannot come in, but the clothes and sandwiches have fallen out, and that anklets around the feet of the horse protect it against the bite of sharks, Dr. Schilder said: "No wonder that persons faced with so much destructive nonsense finally do not know whether they exist or whether they are part of a dream and will vanish."

Bad as this is, the good doctor is not satisfied. He must cite numerous instances of "anxiety" caused by the perusal of Carroll's fantasies and the frightful consequences of this "anxiety" on the childish mind.

"Bottles start to fly," he said. "Candlesticks elongate. A train is jumping over a river. It is an uncertain world. In addition, right and wrong are changed by the mirror. The king's whole army tumbles and falls. So do the Red and the White Knight. Father William balances on his head. There is not much certainty in such a world. One does not wonder that Alice is rather afraid she might be a dream of the Red King.

"Time does not escape distortion. It stands either still or goes even in the opposite direction, although it is even difficult for Carroll to persist with such a distortion for a very long time. One of the letters he wrote to one of his little friends starts with the last word of the letter and finishes with the first, a complete reversal."

He told of Carroll's sin of playing with words and cited such instances as the shoes in the sea being made of soles and eels, the whiting making the shoes and boots white and that no wise fish would go anywhere without porpoise.

Whenever one starts playing with words," he warned, "the problem of negation and the problem of opposites will emerge soon.

He characterized Carroll's condensation of words, such as "mimsy" for flimsy and miserable, as a "ruthless treatment of words, handles without consideration."

"In schizophrenia," he pointed out, "such a treatment of words signifies the wish of the individual to give up definite relations to the world which is after all a world of regular sequences and of meaning."

Dr. Schilder's paper, while approaching the ultimate in utter asininity, is alas, only one instance of the awful stuff habitually turned out in psychiatric literature. Some of these articles are ordinary routine reports and need no embellishments beyond their factual statement, but they read more like the outpourings of the disordered minds which they seek to describe. Few of these writers even know the meaning of the words they employ and the result is to confuse the reader and bewilder the public. While it no doubt ministers to the self-esteem of the writers, it is a wholly useless and destructive performance.

Psychoanalysis is still in a state so nebulous that its advocates cannot afford to sponsor such preposterous outpourings. What little is known along present lines is wholly experimental and may be discarded tomorrow for something entirely different; yet it might conceivably be the means of leading science into the correct path. Why, therefore, expose the embryo to a possible premature death by ridicule?

An unseemly and unreasonable yearning for newspaper publicity seems to be at the bottom of this inhibition. At another similar doctors' meeting a year or two ago, in Toronto, one of their leading lights made the front page in all the papers of the country by proving to his own satisfaction, at least, that Lincoln was a "schizophreniac"—a term invented by Dr. Bleuler, of Zürich, Switzerland, to denote a man with a mind which worked two ways at once. When one considers what Lincoln did, I doubt whether he had only a double-barreled mind. I should imagine it more likely rivaled a machine gun.

In all the literature pertaining particularly to childhood, it should for the present be read with a questioning mind. Occasionally there are some germs of thought that are worth considering, but in the present state of the science it is not wise to accept everything as gospel truth.

How much more instructive and hopeful is the paper read by that distinguished Vienna psychiatrist Dr. Manfeld Sakel. He tells of the beneficent effects of insulin on more than three hundred patients he has treated in the last three years.

Lending their support to Dr. Sakel's conclusions, a number of American brain specialists reported a measure of success in experiments in this country.

> "In cases which run a favorable course, the repeated hypoglycemic states finally eliminate the psychosis, so that the normal personality can again achieve complete dominance."

Others who have experimented with the method, which seeks a cure by reducing sharply the sugar content of the blood, and found it "promising," included Dr. Joseph Wortis, of the psychopathic division of Bellevue Hospital; Dr. Bernard Glueck, medical director of Stony Lodge, Ossining; Dr. John R. Russ, superintendent of the Harlem Valley State Hospital, Wingdale, N.Y., and Dr. W. V. Cline Jr., of the staff of that hospital.

I have heard several conversations along this line and have been greatly impressed with the blood theory. At all events let us have more discussion along this line and less—or none at all—along the "Alice in Wonderland" stuff.

When I say that insanity is preventable and curable in most cases, few men in the medical profession will dispute the assertion. You have, of course, seen Cruden's "Concordance of the Bible." One of the great books of all time. It was compiled by Alexander Cruden, who was adjudged insane at the time. There are, of course, instances in which some malformation of Nature makes this impossible, but this cause is not transmittable. If you've had an uncle or aunt, a father, mother, brother or sister, who has been inflicted in this manner, it stops right there. It is not a trait that you inherit as you do the general family resemblance. It is strictly localized to that one particular case. But thinking of it constantly, dreading it and permitting it to obsess you is very foolish and dangerous. That, however, can be and must be controlled. Put the suggestion absolutely out of your mind and keep it there. The average person has no idea how much harm can be done by simply brooding over a certain fear. What is merely visionary and impalpable speedily becomes a stern and awful reality. So if you are troubled with thoughts of this kind, make up your mind to dismiss them at *once and forever.*

Furthermore, as a result of three years' close contact and constant association with insane persons, I am more than ever convinced that much sickness has its origin in trivial sources never before suspected. Let us consider what a leading member of the American College of Surgeons has to say on the plebeian habit of "getting mad." Isaac Watts, who wrote these lines, familiar to most children,

Let dogs delight to bark and bite,
For God hath made them so;
Let bears and lions growl and fight,
For 'tis their nature too.

But, children, you should never let
Such angry passions rise;
Your little hands were never made
To tear each other's eyes.

may have had in mind only the spiritual aspect of the case, but practical medicine looks at it from a more material point of view. It points out that sudden spasms of anger have a very injurious effect upon the physical system. The change of color in the face, from white to red, or vice versa, indicates that very extensive disarrangements are taking place beneath the surface. Any feeling so powerful as to subtract the blood from one portion of the anatomy or to send it scurrying in unwanted quantities to another, shows that the heart has suddenly experienced a violent strain. Such a happening does not tend to a long life. Laboratory tests prove that persons who let themselves go whenever the impulse moves them, are doing themselves a serious injury. Their excuse that they were born that way and cannot help themselves, is sheer nonsense. We have all known men who allow themselves to get in a towering rage over some very trivial matter. Perhaps if that man knew that he might snap one of the numerous delicate tissues of his brain, causing him to spend his old age in an insane asylum, he might very readily learn to control himself.

As far as my experience went, there was no difficulty in pursuing an intelligent and interesting conversation at all times with most of the patients. If they had any hallucinations or complexes, they succeeded admirably in suppressing them while talking with me. This, I might add, is practically an impossibility. While a mind is out of control, it will wander all over the lot in spite of your best efforts to direct it. So when you converse with a dear friend or relative in one of your visits and he keeps up a sustained conversation with you, it is a positive sign that in due time he will get well. How soon, no one can predict. The period of darkness may be long or short. That is in the laps of the gods, but the fact that he talks rationally should be of the greatest comfort. It proves conclusively that reason is still enthroned. The power to converse intelligently is a positive sign that the patient is getting well. When a patient talks gibberish or makes a noise like a ballyhoo artist in an advertising agency, then there is room for apprehension, but even that state is frequently only temporary, and not permanent, as in agencies.

So on your next visit, come to your friend with a mind full of good cheer and talk light-heartedly. Avoid any reference to mistakes of the past. That is gone and, as I said before, is a dangerous topic to discuss.

Mental health is a priceless possession, but when you consider present day social conditions, the crimes, the delinquencies, the accidents, the terrific strain for mere existence, the quarrels, the vices, the huge task of making both ends meet in these halcyon days of convenient payments; the thousand and one other things that make life a distracting problem, one can readily see that a match lighted near all this gasoline is quite apt to cause an explosion.

Disorders arising from such a condition of affairs may be either physical or mental. When physical, the situation is accepted without much undue excitement; but if mental, then everybody promptly takes leave of what little sense they have.

Mental disease is a dreadful thing; no use denying it. Nor is it being cured entirely. The doctors still know too little about it to be able to do that, but enough has been learned about the nature of this disturbance to rob it of its old time hopelessness and to bring it definitely within the circle of curable medical diseases. That must be so, else the present writer would not be penning these words. Nor would you be interested in reading them if you did not feel that they were written by a man now in possession of all his senses. If you are willing to admit all this, you must be willing to admit that his is not the only case on record of a cure. Having reached this point in your deductions, you may be willing to admit that the man who says insanity is incurable, is possibly wrong.

That public opinion has slowly but surely, during recent years, swung around to this point of view, can no longer be questioned. Increasing numbers now consult the doctor for mental troubles just as they would if they had a dangerous cold, and this admission that is a condition susceptible of treatment just as other diseases, has brought about a vast change in the world of psychiatry. Now that the public understand and appreciate their efforts in this direction, it has spurred them on to further and more intense research.

Better and more far-reaching in its effect would be a still wider recognition, on the part of the public, that insanity is not the dreadfully hopeless thing of legend and story. If it were possible to spread the knowledge everywhere that insanity is just the same as any other sickness, it would place this disease on a common-sense basis and enable the doctors to do their work, not with patients half-crazed with fear and despair; but with men and women who are quite ill, but know they will recover after a reasonable length of treatment.

There are so many different kinds of nervous troubles that it is hard to describe any particular symptom that would warn you that it was time to see a doctor. A very good indication, however, is usually provided by sleeplessness and loss of appetite. When this condition can no longer be ignored, it is time to consult a physician.

This increasing tendency to seek help when the earliest symptoms appear, is something to be greatly encouraged. It is so much easier to check this disease at the beginning than to battle with it when it has once started. Thus, early medical attention is of the greatest importance. Nor does it necessarily follow that when you are sent to an institution you are hopelessly gone. Last year the percentage of those discharged, as cured, from the State Hospitals alone, averaged nearly 30% cured and another 20% so greatly improved as to be able to go home and resume life cautiously. There are committees on Mental Hygiene operating all over the country in conjunction with the National Committee of Hygiene, organized by Mr. Clifford W. Beers, himself a reclaimed patient, and there is a social service provided by the State to help patients get started again after they leave the hospitals.

When your friend goes to a mental hospital, do not let fear grip your heart; do not shake your head ominously and say, "Poor chap, what a pity!" Look at it just as if he had gone to a general hospital for appendicitis, or some minor operation, or to get better attention than he could at home. A few years ago appendicitis, or "inflammation of the bowels," as we called it then, was invariably fatal. So doctors do make progress. Discuss your friend's illness just as you would any other serious topic, but don't get into a blue funk or give everybody the impression that something's happened to your friend worse than death. Be sensible and reasonable and use your head.

To the vast majority of people, State Hospitals for the mentally ill exist only as something they occasionally read about. It is a matter in which they have no personal interest and regard it solely a function of the body politic, like building a new reservoir or widening a river. Very necessary and useful things for the community, but not a matter of any special importance.

Unfortunately, this mental trouble is tremendously on the increase. One of the large insurance companies recently stated in one of its advertisements that in a family of five, one of them would at some time or other suffer from this malady. And until civilization becomes wholly adjusted to the rush and bustle of this machine age, we may look for further additions to the long lists already in our hospitals.

When trouble of this kind enters a family, it is a serious matter. It is the most expensive sickness we have, not only because of its excessively long continuance, but also for the expense of nurses who must be employed and of the necessarily high rates of private sanitariums. The State does all it can and, for the class of people which it is created to serve, does its work admirably. Persons who avail themselves of this public aid are, of course, those whose means are practically nil. To the vast majority of these people, the State Hospital is a marvelous institution. It provides the best of medical care, maintains an adequate nursing staff, and relieves the families of the afflicted of a financial burden that in most cases would prove unsupportable.

PeaceLove

PeaceLove is changing how people think about mental health. PeaceLove provides expressive arts programming to help individuals and communities create peace of mind. They use creative expression to inspire, heal, and communicate emotions that are often difficult to convey in words.

THE CREATORS PROGRAM

PeaceLove programs strive to inspire, educate and build self-confidence through creative expression, inclusion and a message of hope. Through the CREATORS Program, PeaceLove equips front-line professionals to deliver our expressive arts curriculum to communities in need. Facilitators work directly with individuals, families, and groups throughout the country to help them achieve improved mental health and better quality of life through artistic expression.

After receiving training, CREATORS deliver a workshop series consisting of visual arts, storytelling, sound and movement with the purpose of providing new resources and skills to achieve mental wellness.

If you would like more inforamtion, please visit PeaceLove's website at www.peacelove.org.

The Books of Wisdom/Work

Wisdom/Work is a new cooperative, cutting edge imprint and resource for publishing books by practical philosophers and innovative thinkers who can have a positive cultural impact in our time. We turn the procedures of traditional publishing upside down and put more power, a vastly higher speed of delivery, and greater rewards into the hands of our authors.

The imprint was launched with the Morris Institute for Human Values, founded by Tom Morris (Ph.D. Yale), a former professor of philosophy at Notre Dame and a public philosopher who has given over a thousand talks on the wisdom of the ages. Wisdom/Work was established to serve both his audiences and the broader culture. From the imprint's first projects, it began to attract the attention of other authors who seek to expand their positive influence.

Wisdom/Work occupies a distinctive territory outside most traditional publishing domains. Its main concern is high quality expedited production and release, with affordability for buyers. We seek to serve a broad audience of intelligent readers with the best of ancient and modern wisdom. Subjects will touch on such issues as success, ethics, happiness, meaning, work, and how best to live a good life.

As an imprint, we have created a process for working with a few high quality projects a year compatible with our position in the market, and making available to our authors a well-guided and streamlined process for launching their books into the world. For more information, email Tom Morris, Editor-in-Chief, through his reliable address of: TomVMorris@aol.com. You can also learn more at the editor's website, www.TomVMorris.com.